IRON HEART PUBLISHING

ABUBILAAL YAKUB

THE
CRUCIBLE
OF
ABSTINENCE

IRONHEART
PUBLISHING HOUSE

ISBN-13: 978-1-989450-18-5

Published by Iron-Heart Publishing.

www.ironheartpublishing.com

The purpose of this study is purely for an ambition of knowledge and enlightenment.

The contents of this book do not represent a universal view, because a universal view is not absolute and evident. No part of this book is an attempt at predicting or discerning future events or outcomes, nor is there an intent to impose views, doctrines, or ideologies.

We do acknowledge that there may be other intellectual views more accurate and authentic than ours, in which case, we encourage active participation and correspondence through channels enlisted at the end of the book.

Kindly approach this book and its contents with an open mind and an open heart. If a difference of opinion arises, we encourage the reader to do an impartial and objective study so as to present an alternate view by which both the reader and the author can benefit.

الحمد لله رب العالمين

وصلاة والسلام على خاتم النبيين

سيد المرسلين ، محمد الأمين ، وعلى آله وصحابته أجمعين

اللهم لا علم لنا إلا ما علمتنا إنك أنت العليم الحكيم

اللهم علمنا ما ينفعنا وانفعنا بما علمتنا و زدنا علما

اللهم ارزق علينا فهم النبيين وحفظ المرسلين

اللهم افتح علينا حكمتك وانشر علينا رحمتك

ياذا الجلال والإكرام

In the name of God Almighty, the Most Merciful, the Most Gracious, whose Divine Majesty perplexes the Hearts and Minds of many a great people. In the Hearts of our Beloved Prophets, His Light guides them to guide us. In the Hearts of the Enlightened Scholars of Islām, esteemed as they are, His Light guides the Prophets to guide them.
We are all but slaves and servants to His Greatness.
Like the thirsty in the desert, I yearn for every droplet of Knowledge, from the Holy Prophet of Almighty Allāh to the Enlightened Scholars of Islām all to whom I dedicate this book.

Lastly...
To my beloved wife, Shaheena Yakub.

May Allāh Almighty shower you all with His Mercy and Blessings, and bestow upon you a high rank and a special place in Jannat-ul-Firdaus.

Ameen

Ever did I deem the insignificance of my being,

Never to esteem the vast realms within,

And the absurdity to infer a thing to be just a thing,

Never to truly see reality from what it merely seems,

Cast into a meaningless chasm, and consumed therein,

What does my being fulfill? What legacy will I depart?

Is there any true worth in that which I impart?

Is there a reward in those dreams or that life, in whole or in part?

For when will I realize what it truly means,

Dreams are shattered when the Self politics against the Will of the Heart,

In those dreams I saw that life was benign,

When awake I saw that servitude was its design,

But only when I served did I taste the felicity of its wine,

Here I found a dream worth living and a life worthy of dreams,

And thus did it dawn, that all I had to do was seek the Divine...

CONTENTS

يَوْمَ لَا يَنفَعُ مَالٌ وَلَا بَنُونَ إِلَّا مَنْ أَتَى ٱللَّهَ بِقَلْبٍ سَلِيمٍ

Then on that Day, naught will benefit of Wealth or Legacy,

Save he who comes to Allāh with a Sound Heart

~ *Sūrah Ash-Shu'arā 26:88-89* ~

WHO ARE YOU

We begin, as ever, with the glorious name of Allāh, the Most Merciful, the Most Benevolent. And we send salutations of peace and blessings upon His noble messenger and his kin, the rightly-guided companions, and all the esteemed scholars borne of his guidance, from whose fingertips we drink the sweet nectar of knowledge and enlightenment.

O' Beloved...

Who are you? *What* are you?

You masquerade yourself smart and prosperous as you crusade an ambition to attain the mark of success. Flourishing and thriving a job or career, conquering arbitrary milestones to reach the heights of mundane recognition. Celebrating a sensory joy traded with currency as you measure your worth by the numbers accrued in your vaults. Watching that joy turned to sorrow the moment the numbers dwindle. Lost awash on the shores of despair when seas of frivolity and vanity toss you asunder. You are so remarked by the meager regressions

15

of modernity posed as 'advancements,' so spellbound by the complexities of the systems and schematics of modernity that you fail to see the spawning monster within. Words like 'modern' and 'technology' enthrall you into a state of ecstasy. You strive to seek the marvel of every new craft and technique, anticipating a temporal sense of glee, until it decays away to leave you empty and void. Then you despair. You abandon faith and hope. For what goes up must come down, every beginning has an end, and you are unrealizing to the temporality of life. Unrealizing to its acrimonious tempestuousness.

Who are you really then? What are you then, but a follower of whimsical conventionalities established by benighted minds that are far removed from the Divine Presence? What are you then, but an empty husk that sways with the wind, with nothing absolute to believe in?

Did you once, in your life, halt from its inescapable turbulences to contemplate your *being?* To depart from the noise you so assumed was 'normal,' never once debating its abnormality. Did you ever pause to reflect on your existence? From whence did you come? To where are you headed?

Who are you *really?*

If you did not, you have forgone the very purpose of your breath. If you did, what resulted from your considerations and deliberations? Did you find the answers you sought? Did you realize the majesty of your quintessent self-hood, or did you simply assume then that you originated in jest or at random? A desultory juxtaposition of biological matter. Something without a purpose, a bearing or heading. Something that simply ate, drank, slept, and entertained to *be* entertained. Or did you sense deep down, somewhere in the fathoms of your veiled reality, that there was more to you?

When you thus thought, or thought you thought, in your suppositions and their deliberations, guided and sustained by the godless in whom you placed your trust of truth, that your life was but a life, a meaningless, frivolous, useless thing, a comeuppance in amusement, pointless to the point of self ambition, something that was done in play or jest, a by-the-by.

What is it to see the world in a grain of sand, and heaven in a flower? What is it to hold Infinity in the palm of your hand, and embrace eternity in an hour?[1]

Nay, but you were marvelously conceived in a sacred crucible, delicately unraveled by a Graceful Hand, from marvelous means to a profound destiny, and at great end for great purpose. That although you are not from the everlasting, you will indeed last forever; and though your body is mean, fragile, and earthly, your spirit is lofty and divine.

When thus placed in the Crucible of Abstinence, you are purged from your carnal passions, attaining to the highest. Your sanctum elevated, your noumenon enlightened, and in place of being a slave to lust and anger, you become endued with angelic qualities.

This, the book you hold in your hands, articulates the spiritual alchemy that will morph you from within, like that which turns metal into gold and earth into gems, which is itself not easily unveiled, nor found in a random tome. It is availed only in the treasuries of God, in that which He reveals to the hearts of the Prophets (peace and blessings be upon them all) and in the souls of the righteous and the pious, and thus he who seeks it elsewhere will find only a mirage in the desert, a desolate speck of dust in a void, and will descry himself discontent and disappointed, wasted on the Day of Certainty, the Day of Reckoning, when he hears the words;

لَّقَدْ كُنتَ فِى غَفْلَةٍ مِّنْ هَذَا فَكَشَفْنَا عَنكَ غِطَآءَكَ فَبَصَرُكَ ٱلْيَوْمَ حَدِيدٌ

Indeed you were heedless of this. Thus we have lifted the veils from you so your sight on this Day is piercing [2]

And to forewarn you of that helpless state, when all that

---

1   William Blake, *Auguries of Innocence.* p.1863

2   Sūrah Qāf 50:22

you assumed of your being as truth was but a delusion, and when thus the delusions are lifted and you see with certainty what you should have seen before that moment of truth, He Almighty presents a clear truth forehand;

$$أَفَحَسِبْتُمْ أَنَّمَا خَلَقْنَاكُمْ عَبَثًا وَأَنَّكُمْ إِلَيْنَا لَا تُرْجَعُونَ$$

Did you then assume that We created you without purpose, that you would not be returned to Us?[3]

Further to which He says;

$$أَيَحْسَبُ الْإِنسَانُ أَن يُتْرَكَ سُدًى$$

Does man think that he will be left neglected?[4]

That he will not be questioned? Not held accountable for that which he does and that which he conceals? That every moment of his existence is in effect a debt that must be paid, a debt that *will* be paid, willingly or unwillingly. Does he then delude himself into thinking he is master of his being? Or master of the universe, as he so pines to be?

Where then do all your ambitions and aspirations lie? Where do your allegiances lie? To whom do you truly answer? From whom do you seek the truth? In whose language do you think? Whose thoughts project your world-view?

What did you predicate was the Meaning of Life and the Purpose of Life?

Know then, the hardest truth you will ever know. It is death that unveils the meaning of life. For you are a being temporal in existence, wherewith you will live and will also die, try as you might to ignore the truth of that finality. And ignorant you will remain to that truth, for it will only be unveiled to you should you seek it while you are alive, or await that moment when your final breath departs and death itself unveils it unto you.

---

3   Sūrah al-Muʾminūn 23:115

4   Al-Qiyāmah 75:36

You were sent... yes indeed, you were *sent* into this world, into this life, and that sending was intended, and thus has a purpose. You were not conceived at random, portentously decided upon or chosen by any earthly being. That your birth was not a preferential matter deliberated between those who bore you, for even if they were to have restrained themselves, your birth as ordained will have occurred. Elsewhere, perhaps. To another, perhaps. But born nonetheless, for He Almighty ordained it, and none can counter His ordinance.

What then is the nature of this realm whence you have arrived? What is your purpose in this world? Why this world?

قَالَ اهْبِطُوا بَعْضُكُمْ لِبَعْضٍ عَدُوٌّ ۖ وَلَكُمْ فِى الْأَرْضِ مُسْتَقَرٌّ وَمَتَاعٌ إِلَىٰ حِينٍ

[Allāh] said, "Descend, being to one another enemies. And for you on the earth is a place of settlement and gratification [provision] for a time." [5]

قَالَ فِيهَا تَحْيَوْنَ وَفِيهَا تَمُوتُونَ وَمِنْهَا تُخْرَجُونَ
He said, "Therein you will live, and therein you will die, and from thence you will be brought forth." [6]

Know then, that your defined parameters in this world are that you are to live here, and you are to die here, and from here you will depart. We ask then, if you were sent here, where did you come from? If you will depart here, where are you to go? And if you are here, why *are* you here?

We respond to this by saying that you die because you live, and thus you live so you can die. Which is to say that the reason you are alive is so you can die, for without life you could not have come here, and without death you cannot depart. What is it that is alive then? And what is it that dies?

Know then, that you are not your body, nor your soul, nor your thoughts and emotions, nor your mind, nor your heart,

5   Sūrah Al-A'rāf 7:24

6   Sūrah Al-A'rāf 7:25

nor your will, nor your consciousness. For if these were you, then they would not be 'yours.' You would not say "my body" or "my soul" or "my heart." Indeed, these are all your belongings, extensions of you. They have been bestowed upon you for a reason, to the fulfillment of your purpose. You must affirm this absolute truth, for without it, you cannot proceed in knowing your 'self' or your 'heart'. You must affirm this in defiance of all that is heralded from the godless world and all their sciences and confounded suppositions. They are themselves deluded. Do not associate with the deluded. Associate with the enlightened, the Prophets and the Word of God.

You are the *Being*.

And you, the Being, has been wrapped in a Consciousness with which to affirm or negate reality. And this Consciousness is placed in the Will with which to choose and enact. And this Will is to be found in the true Intellect with which to rationalize and to know. And this Intellect is encased in the Heart with which to understand, contemplate, and thus govern your Being. And this Heart is placed in the Soul, a protecting ethereal substance capable of dwelling between the Realms Spiritual and the Realm Material. And your Soul is thus encrusted into this material, biological body, whose senses and organs enable you, the Being, to experience reality, to be *alive*.

Thus did Imām Ali bin AbīTalib say;

دَواؤُكَ فيكَ وَما تُبصِرُ

وَدَاؤُكَ مِنكَ وَما تَشعُرُ

أَتَزعُمُ أَنَّكَ جُرمٌ صَغيرٌ

وَفيكَ انطَوَى العَالَمُ الأَكبَرُ

Your medicine is in you, if only you would see it,
And your medicine is from you, if only you would feel it,
You think yourself an insignificant thing,
Yet within you reside great worlds,

20

This is the allegory we will hence use. For this great realm that encompasses us is the macrocosm. And the human being is the microcosm to it.

The Body is, in this allegory, the world, for the body is of *this* world. It is that which has a natural function, a set algorithm, preprogrammed to operate as a perfect system. It is itself unintelligent for it is unaware of its existence. It follows sensory inputs, computations, and actuated outputs, which are simple enough to understand however complex their algorithms may be. It is the *Mulk* مُلك , the dominion, with defined boundaries and parameters, which it cannot surpass.

The Soul is its law, that which governs the body in the same way that the laws of the cosmos are collectively the soul of the cosmos. Herein we find the marvel of the soul. That it has two dimensions, reflecting the two aspects of law and order. The lower dimension reflects worldly law, the root of its desires and the base of its moods. It is that which governs the agents of consumption and copulation, which if left ungoverned corrupt the natural order, and the agents of conflict and collision, which also if left ungoverned destroy the natural order. Then there is the higher dimension that reflects Divine Law, the intellection that sits in judgment over the lower dimensions. It is this law that disciplines the rudimentary self.

Reflected here is the purpose of the *Sharī'ah*, the Divine ordinance entrusted to man, whose sole purpose is to discipline the Soul, and we find that this *Sharī'ah* is intended for the intellective dimension, with which it governs the lower dimension.

Then we find that the nature of the world is cyclical, not linear. It is such that Time ordained for this world unravels existence in a cyclical continuum. And in every cycle is ordained a sanctum, a *Crucible*, and this is likened to the Heart. We also find that the motion of Time ordained for the rightly-guided follows not the Solar cycle but the Lunar cycle. And this is because the Solar cycle has been ordained for the *Mulk*. The Body. The dominion. The physical and material. But the

21

Lunar cycle has been ordained for the Ethereal. The Soul. The
Heart. And in this Lunar cycle there is a crucible. A sanctum.
We know it as the *Month of Ramadhān*. The month in which
the Being consciously detaches from the lower dimension. *This*
is the Crucible of Abstinence for the cosmos. What then is the
Crucible of Abstinence for the Being?

It is the Heart.

Concerning the Heart then; it has only two objectives.
These define the Heart in its purpose of creation.

The first is to 'Believe.' The Heart *must* believe. It *must* have
a conviction. Something true and real it can cling to. Such is
the nature of the Heart, that it is clingy. It becomes attached. It
detests separation. It knows that it is helpless. It knows that it
is suspended in such a state of existence that it cannot explain,
nor can it explain how it came to exist, due to which it cannot
know if it will remain in existence or momentarily depart. It
cannot know what unfolds next in its continuum, and this lack
of knowing is its greatest agitation. And due to this agitation,
it wants to cling, to hold on to something that will give it some
surety, some tranquility. We call this تطمئن القلب, the Heart's
assured conviction attained through the remembrance of God.[7]
It is a firm belief that transcends rationality and penetrates the
Heart, settling therein to keep it tranquil. Belief, we say, is an
inherent quality. *What* we believe in will determine the truth of
the belief.

The second of this is contingent on the first. It is to 'Know.'
There is what the Heart knows, what it needs to know, and
what it wants to know. And what it knows is that it does
not truly know. It can recognize its lack of knowing, for it
recognizes its helplessness, and it understands that the only
way it can sustain itself is with knowledge. This seems a strange
notion, but it is a profound truth. For the heart knows that
its helplessness is due to its distance from the Divine Presence
that sustains it, and to return to that Divine Presence is its only
hope for survival, which is only possible through *knowing* the

---

7   Sūrah Ar-Ra'd 13:28

Divine Presence in a state of knowing that is deepest in true understanding. We call this *Ma'rifah* معرفة. It is a knowing that transcends the rationale of particularity and multiplicity, and penetrates the Heart, settling therein with a sound knowing of Unity that cannot be shaken with doubt. And 'knowing' is thus an inherent quality. *What* we know will determine the truth of the knowledge.

More on these two in chapter 7, إن شاء الله. But for now, understand that both of these must be present in the Heart to complement each other. The Heart is only sound when Knowledge and Belief are harmonized internally. There are those who say "We believe" but do not seek knowledge. These are ignorant fools. Then there are those who say "We have knowledge" but do not have a conviction in God. These are heedless husks. For knowledge, in its rightful pursuit, must lead you to know the Lord Almighty. He is the ultimate truth worthy of knowing. And likewise, Faith, in its rightful conviction, must be justified in truth. One cannot be said to have faith, if he does not even know what he believes in.

I therefore hold the following principle. Remember it. Memorize it. Etch it into your heart.

الإيمان بدون العلم جهلا وغفلا

فالغفلة يخف الإعتقاد

والجهل يصغر المعرفة

وهما ظلمات الحزن والشقي

Faith without Knowledge is ignorance and heedlessness,
And heedlessness reduces conviction
And ignorance diminishes knowledge
And both are the darkness of agitation and anguish

Your state of agitation, your depression, your anxiety, your sadness, your lack of motivation, everything you deem as a source of wretchedness in your life, is not some 'psychological' distress, some complex or disorder. You do not need the pills, the recreational drugs, the sensational motivational talks that caress your self-esteem, or the counseling that soothes your feelings, or whatever else they prescribe to you. There is nothing wrong with you other than the wrong you commit. There is no injustice other than the injustice you do unto yourself. By not being the *being* that *He* wants you to be. No one can rectify you. You must take the responsibility for your own wellbeing. Physically. Psychologically. Spiritually.

The seat of all your spiritual states is in your Heart. It is the Sultan that governs your dominion, the vessel of knowledge and understanding, the prime genesis of your being. All you ever need to do is cultivate a soundness in your heart. Give it the absolute assurance it craves. Feed it with the melody and harmony of Divine Ordinance. Nūrture your heart, and you will thus Nūrture your life. Your Heart is a Crucible of Abstinence. Safeguard it from the delusions and distractions of causality, so that it can safeguard you from their turbulences. This is its ordained mission. But it can only fulfill this mission if it is itself sound, and it will only be sound when it has rectified itself. And *that* is why you have been prescribed a period in time, a month that reflects upon the heart as a crucible of abstinence, in which the Heart can cultivate its soundness.

And just as it is in the month of *Ramadhān* that God Almighty chose to reveal the Truth, His Speech, to the most beloved of all, His messenger, in its most inner sanctum, the Night of Divine Power, likewise it is in the innermost dimensions of the heart where one's true meanings are unveiled. These are only arrived at through deep thought, contemplation, and reflection, in the same way that we affirm *Ramadhān* to be a time of reflection. This reflection is only truly achieved when there is an abstinence, a detachment from the material world, from worldly affairs and affiliations, just as the only way to truly reflect on one's self is by detaching from it and its sensory links.

24

For what is the nature of this world but a distraction to the Being? The Being is not of this world, and therefore this is not its true reality. It is an inherent property of the Being that it is ever seeking the Truth, which itself, in its absolute state, exists only with the Absolute. This world is thus a veil of delusion and illusion, perfectly designed to distract the Being in a true test of the Being's power, granted to him by the Almighty.

And He says;

اَعْلَمُوٓا۟ أَنَّمَا ٱلْحَيَوٰةُ ٱلدُّنْيَا لَعِبٌ وَلَهْوٌ وَزِينَةٌ وَتَفَاخُرٌ بَيْنَكُمْ وَتَكَاثُرٌ فِى ٱلْأَمْوَٰلِ وَٱلْأَوْلَٰدِ ۖ كَمَثَلِ غَيْثٍ أَعْجَبَ ٱلْكُفَّارَ نَبَاتُهُۥ ثُمَّ يَهِيجُ فَتَرَىٰهُ مُصْفَرًّا ثُمَّ يَكُونُ حُطَٰمًا ۖ وَفِى ٱلْءَاخِرَةِ عَذَابٌ شَدِيدٌ وَمَغْفِرَةٌ مِّنَ ٱللَّهِ وَرِضْوَٰنٌ ۚ وَمَا ٱلْحَيَوٰةُ ٱلدُّنْيَآ إِلَّا مَتَٰعُ ٱلْغُرُورِ

Know that the life of this world is play, and amusement, and luxury [leisure] and boasting, and competition in wealth and progeny. Like the rain that pleases the farmers crop. Thereafter it dries and turns yellow. Thereafter it withers to dust. And in the Hereafter, there is grave punishment, and there is forgiveness from Allāh and pleasure. And not is the life of this world but an enjoyment of delusion.[8]

We thus end this chapter with the words of a true servant of the Almighty;

الأكوان ظاهرها غرّة ، وباطنها عبرة ، فالنفس تنظر إلى ظاهر غرتها، و القلب ينظر إلى باطن عبرتها

The world is in its outward a distraction, but in its inward a discernment; for the soul looks at its outward distraction; and the heart sees its inward discernment.[9]

---

8   Sūrah Al-Hadīd 57:20

9   *Al-Hikam Al-'Ata'iyyah;* Ibn Ata'illah Al-Iskandary

25

You then, the Being, must decide. Are you one to follow the inclinations of your indisciplined soul and remain transfixed on the distractions until your time has run its course? Or are you one to filter the blemishes and turn your heart's gaze to discern true reality which takes you closer to the truth. Are you one to unravel your purpose and the meaning of your life consciously? Or are you one to remain distracted in the fleeting moments of material bliss until that one moment when the meaning of life is finally unveiled to you, but there is nothing you can do about it then?

You are the Being. The choice is always and only yours.

THE HEART

Knowing the heart cannot be done without first knowing that which has been tasked to vessel the heart. The carrier that acts both as the heart's asset and equally its liability. That which is spiritual cannot survive in the material, and that which is material cannot survive the spiritual, these being two entities at complete ends of the spectrum of existence. The being has been sent into the material realm, given a material body, but the being itself is spiritual. And the spiritual cannot fuse with the material without one annihilating the other, much in the same way that two objects cannot blend unless there is a destruction between them— or a catalyst that can bind them.

This catalyst is called 'Aether' or that which is 'Ethereal.' This is the Soul. It is a unique entity that can bind to the spiritual in one aspect, and bind to the material in another aspect, thereby playing the mediating role, in this case, between the heart that is of pure essence, and the body that is of pure matter.

If we say that the key to knowing the Creator is the heart, then the key to knowing the heart is the soul, and the key to knowing the soul is the self. The 'self' is thus the characteristics, the qualities, the nature of the soul. This is what AbūHāmid Al-Ghazzālī elaborates in these two sections extracted from his marvelous treatise entitled 'The Alchemy of Happiness.'

[I have placed the Arabic text in segments followed by my own translation, and my commentary and explanation of each section is in the footnotes]

فصل في معرفة النفس
On Knowing the Self

اعلم أن مفتاح معرفة الله تعالى هو معرفة النفس، كما قال

سبحانه وتعالى : سَنُرِيهِمْ ءَايَـٰتِنَا فِى ٱلْأَفَاقِ وَفِىٓ أَنفُسِهِمْ حَتَّىٰ يَتَبَيَّنَ لَهُمْ أَنَّهُ ٱلْحَقُّ

Know then, that the key to knowing Almighty Allāh is knowing the 'self', as He has said, Glory unto Him; {We will show them Our Signs on the horizons and in them [their] selves, until it becomes manifestly clear that it [His word] is the truth}[10]

وقال النبي صلى الله عليه وسلم: من عرف نفسه فقد عرف ربه

And the Prophet, peace and blessings be upon him said, {whosoever knows his self, knows his Lord}.[11]

وليس شيء أقرب إليك من نفسك، فإذا لم تعرف نفسك، فكيف تعرف ربك؟

And there is nothing closer to you than your 'self.' For if you do not even know yourself, how are you to know your Lord?[12]

---

10 Sūrah Fussilat 41:53. The *Ufuq* أفق symbolizes the meeting place the horizon بين السماوات والأرض between the Heavens and the Earth. Likewise, the Soul is an entity created and placed between the realms spiritual and the realm material. It serves the intermediary, the catalyst between these two realms, between the Body الجسم, and the Spirit الروح.

11 This is not a Hadīth of the Prophet by consensus of Hadīth Scholars. There is no chain of narration, no attribution directly to him. However, some scholars have used it as a Hadīth, while others take it as a proverb since its meaning is sound in truth and wisdom. See my commentary on Ghazzālī's *Kimyā as-Sa'ādah*, entitled *Ghazzālī's Alchemy of Happiness*, for a detailed explanation.

12 This is a summation of that saying. To know your Lord, you must be endowed with purity in your Heart. A pure heart is granted the *Nūr* نور with which to know the Creator. It can only be purified if its vessel, the Soul is purified. To purify the Heart, therefore, you must purify the Soul. And to purify the Soul, you must first know the Soul. Know its strengths and its weaknesses. In knowing yourself, you come to know your Heart. In knowing your Heart, you come to know He who created the Heart.

فإن قلت: إني أعرف نفسي! فإنما تعرف الجسم الظاهر، الذي هو اليد والرجل
والرأس والجثة، ولا تعرف ما في باطنك من الأمر الذي به إذا غضبت طلبت
الخصومة، وإذا اشتهيت طلبت النكاح، وإذا جعت طلبت الأكل، وإذا عطشت
طلبت الشرب. والدواب تشاركك في هذه الأمور.

*So if you were to claim, "I know myself!" You but only know
your physical body, that which (manifests as) the hands, the legs,
the head, and the torso. But you do not know what is your inward
(reality) from issuance of that which prompts it, when you are
irate you seek to argue, when you lust you seek copulation, when
you hunger you seek to consume, when you thirst you seek drink.
And the beasts share these issuances with you.*[13]

فالواجب عليك أن تعرف نفسك بالحقيقة؛
حتى تدرك أي شيء أنت، ومن أين جئت إلى هذا المكان، ولأي شيء خلقت،
وبأي شيء سعادتك، وبأي شيء شقاؤك

It is an obligation upon you to know yourself in reality;

*Until you realize what you are. Wherefrom did you come to
arrive at this destination. And of what you have been created.
And which is it that will bring you felicity. And which is it that
will bring you damnation.*

---

13 Science in modernity holds the stubborn position that the only
existing entity is the body because other than that nothing else
can be 'empirically' proven, in that the assumption is everything
about the human being is but a biological function, actions and
reactions of catabolic and anabolic states. Most, if asked, if they
know themselves, will instinctively assume so, oblivious that
all they really know is their biological composition, something
that is already likened to beasts and animals. This is the flawed
Epistemology of modern science that seeks to arrive at the human
being's existential truth through the channels of biological
investigations. When asked about the psychology of the being, they
presume to have profound knowledge, yet all they can avail are
behaviors and traits, mere symptoms and manifestations of a reality
that cannot be quantified empirically. For where does the ability of
the consciousness to affirm and negate come from? Where do the
thoughts and emotions reside? Where does the will to decide come
from? These inclinations, these reactions to psychological stimuli,
where do they originate?

وقد جمعت في باطنك صفات: منها صفات البهائم، ومنها صفات السباع، ومنها صفات الشياطين، ومنها صفات الملائكة، فالروح حقيقة جوهرك وغيرها غريب منك، وعارية عندك، فالواجب عليك أن تعرف هذا، وتعرف أن لكل واحد من هؤلاء غذاء وسعادة

فإن سعادة البهائم في الأكل، والشرب، والنوم، والنكاح، فإن كنت منهم فاجتهد في أعمال الجوف والفرج

وسعادة السباع في الضرب، والفتك

وسعادة الشياطين في المكر، والشر، والحيل. فإن كنت منهم فاشتغل باشتغالهم وسعادة الملائكة في مشاهدة جمال الحضرة الربوبية، وليس للغضب والشهوة إليهم طريق. فإن كنت من جوهر الملائكة، فاجتهد في معرفة أصلك؛ حتى تعرف الطريق إلى الحضرة الإلهية، وتبلغ إلى مشاهدة الجلال والجمال، وتخلص نفسك من قيد الشهوة والغضب، وتعلم أن هذه الصفات لأي شيء ركبت فيك؛ فما خلقها الله تعالى لتكون أسيرها، ولكن خلقها حتى تكون أسرك، وتسخرها للسفر الذي قدامك، وتجعل إحداها مركبك، والأخرى سلاحك؛ حتى تصيد بها سعادتك

And thus collected within you (your 'self') are certain qualities. From among them are bestial (ruminant) qualities; and predatory qualities; and demonic qualities; and Angelic qualities.

And the spirit is the reality of your essence, and anything other than that is alienated from it. It is of the utmost importance that you know this. And (likewise) that each of these qualities is there to facilitate your felicity.

For the contentment of the beasts is in consumption, and drink, and sleep, and copulation. If you are from these, then strive in the efforts of the stomach and the genitals.[14]

---

14 This is the quality of Ruminance, from Latin *Ruminare* meaning 'to chew the cud' i.e to consume. Beasts, typically livestock and hoofed animals, or herbivores both wild and domesticated, are called Ruminants, because their inherent nature is concerned only with consumption and copulation. This quality is reflected in the human being as his Concupiscence شهوة, the base of which is a lust of sensual satisfaction.

And the contentment of the predators is in confrontation and hostility.[15]

And the contentment of the demons is in deceit, stratagem, plotting and planning, shrewdness and cunningness. So if you are from these, then endeavor in these endeavors.[16]

But the contentment of the Angels is in witnessing the beauty of the Lordly Presence, and irascibility and concupiscence are not from their way. So if you are from the angelic essence, then strive in knowing your origin; until you come to know the path to the Divine Presence. And you arrive at witnessing the Beauty and Majesty. And you rid your 'self' of the irascibility and the concupiscence. And you come to know why these were assembled in you. For not did Almighty Allāh create them that you be imprisoned by them, rather He created them that they may facilitate your journey, and to make use of them for the journey before you, and to place one of them as your riding beast, and the other as your weapon, until you capture your felicity.

---

15 Likewise, 'predator' from its Latin *Praedari* meaning 'seized as plunder' relates to creatures that kill and reap without consequence. Their nature is harshness, cruelty, violence, and brutality. This quality is reflected in the human being as his Irascibility غضب. Such people are prone to argumentations, reactions, foolhardiness, vulgarity. They are very defensive, both psychologically and physically, and are ever eager to dispute and contend with others.

16 The standard delusion is that *Shayatīn* شياطين are only from the Jinn, hence whenever 'Shaytaan' is mentioned, the direct implication is assumed to be other than human. But *Shaytān* شيطان does not mean Jinn. It means Demon, and as such any part of creation can become Demonic. This quality is manifest when both the Concupiscence and Irascibility have overridden the Intellect, and likewise, the Intellect itself is acting on its own accord without regulation by the Heart and Guidance from the Divine. Such people are prone to deceit, conceit, deviousness, plotting and planning, strategizing, and the likes thereof.

فصل كيف تعرف نفسك؟

How would you know the Self?

إذا شئتَ أن تعرف نفسك، فاعلم أنك من شيئين

الأول: هذا القلب

والثاني: يسمى النفس والروح

If you wish to know yourself, then know that you (in your
inward) are of two things;
The first is the Heart.
The second you would call the Soul and the Spirit.[17]

والنفس هو القلب الذي تعرفه بعين الباطن

And the soul is the "heart" with which with you understand
as the 'Inward Eye.' [18]

---

17 This distinction is important to make. The first is the central
faculty, the Heart. The second is what lies on either "side" of the
heart. On the one, there is the soul, and that is the Heart's link
to the created realm, or the material world (of the body). On the
other, there is the spirit, and that is the Heart's link to the spiritual
realm. There is no tangible or formal representation of these entities
as they are not material. This is the closest in linear representation
that we can render. Here the heart has two inroads of knowledge,
that which is acquired externally from sensoria and intellection,
and that which is divinely inspired through revelation.

18 The 'Inner Eye' is the eye of reason, the eye of intellection, the
eye that sees an essential reality of *meaning*. There are those who
argue that this a physical component found in the brain as the
Pineal Gland. They are wrong, and much of what they argue is
sourced from the symbolism of conspiracy theories. The 'Inner Eye'
cannot be regarded as a material component. Factually, an eye can
only 'see' when light enters it. If this inner eye, per their arguments,
is located somewhere within the biological body, such as the brain,
they should also explain how light manages to penetrate bone,
muscle, tissue, and brain matter to enter the pineal gland. We say
that the inner eye is immaterial, and a component of ethereal body,
such as is explained by Ghazzali as the Heart. Its light is therefore
also immaterial. It is Divine Light that we know as *Nūr*. And the
Nūr of Divinity is not something emitted by the Sun or the Stars
or that bulb in your room. You will understand this better when we
come to Chapter 6.

وحقيقتك الباطن؛

And your true reality is inward.[19]

لأن الجسد أول وهو الآخر، والنفس آخر وهو الأول. ويسمى قلبا

*Because the body is the first, and it (the Heart) is the last.
And the soul is the last, and it (the heart) is the first.*[20]

وليس القلب هذه القطعة اللحمية التي في الصدر من الجانب الأيسر؛ لأنه يكون

في الدواب والموتى

*It is called the Heart. And the Heart is not this mound of
flesh that is in the chest inclining to the left. Because this is also
in beasts and corpses.*[21]

---

19 The word 'reality' here must be understood in the essential
meaning of the term حقيقة, which means *'True Reality'* distinct from
a material reality denoted by the term واقعية, which means 'realistic'
or 'factual reality.' In the English language, the word 'reality' should
be rendered in the same connotation as the term واقعية, not حقيقة. In
other words, what the secular world defines as reality is a material,
factual, causal-effectual reality. This returns to the etymology of
the word in the Latin 'Res' which means matter, thing, goods, or
property. Thus, when asked for the nature of reality, modernity will
idealize only the physicality of things. Islām challenges this notion,
that foremost reality is not just the state of what things actually are,
it is what God ordains them to be, which in their realities, extends
to their Ontological and Teleological states as well. In Islām, the
term حقيقة comes from حق, hence it directly pertains Truth. Truth
cannot be what creation supposes it to be. Truth is what God says
is Truth, which is why one of His Divine Attributes is الحق. Reality
thus relates to *True* Reality, or a reality higher than a material reality.

20 This must be understood in the Arabic. What it essentially
means is that the Body is the first, outwardly perceived, but the
Heart supersedes it. And that the soul is the last inwardly perceived,
but the heart exceeds it. In other words, the Heart is both the first
and the last. It was the first entity created for the being, and upon
death, it will carry on, for it resides with the being in the entirety
of its existence. Here you must understand that upon creating you
as the *being,* the Almighty created the Heart in which you were
placed. The Heart was then given the soul to enable it to merge
with the body that was fashioned for it. Upon death, the soul
bearing the heart is removed from the body. From thence, it is the
heart that endures.

21 Ghazzali is referring to the True Heart, by way of saying that
this beating organ is but a symbolic, or 'formal' representation of
the Heart itself. The physical heart reacts when the spiritual heart
is joyous or sorrowful. The physical heart also decays with disease
when the spiritual heart is diseased.

وكل شيء تبصره بعين الظاهر فهو من هذا العالم الذي يسمى عالم الشهادة

And everything that you see with your outward eye[22] *is from this realm, which is called the 'Observable Realm.'*[23]

وأما حقيقة القلب، فليس من هذا العالم، لكنه من عالم الغيب؛ فهو في هذا العالم غريب وتلك القطعة اللحمية مركبة

As for the reality of the Heart, it is not from this realm.[24] *It is, in this realm, a stranger, and the mound of flesh (the organ) is a vessel.*[25]

––––––––––––––

22   Physical Eyes, which is inclusive of all sensory perception. The human being has five perceptive senses which are the eyes, nose, ears, tongue, and skin. Further to which there are receptive senses which include the organs. The eyes are the most powerful of the perceptive sense, for visual perception provides a much broader content of information. This is why, in a manner of speaking, 'sight' or 'seeing' is often inclusive of sense perception.

23   I have translated it literally, but in our contemporary speech, the *'ālam ash-Shahādah* عالم الشهادة would be the "observable universe." In other words, anything that is observable through sensoria, even by the use of instrumentation, is a composite of the physical material universe. This includes all that is Quantum. Now, some will debate the use of the term "universe" with the claim that عالم means "realm" not "universe." We would reconcile this by saying that the term "universe" is a contemporary term, whose origins are placed around the 1500s. The word 'Universe' comes from its Latin roots of *Unus* meaning 'One' and *Versus* meaning 'Turned' or 'Transformed,' which renders the term as 'combined into one'. The sinister idea behind such a definition is that whatever is assumed to be 'spiritual' is condensed into one form which conveniently happens to be a material form. The Holy Qurān challenges this notion by repeatedly stating that the Spiritual and Material realms are distinct through the phrase السماوات والأرض, *the Heavens and the Material World.*

24   Because it is not a material thing, and cannot be observed using sense perception. The spiritual heart cannot be seen, touched, or heard sensorially and physically, hence it cannot be empirically observed and measured.

25   Which does not mean that if the physical heart is cut open, one will find the spiritual heart tucked inside. As a "vessel" it simply means where the Heart establishes itself when then soul is breathed into the body. The mind establishes itself in the Brain, the Concupiscence establishes itself in the Stomach and Genitals, and the Irascible establishes itself in the Liver and the Limbs.

وكل أعضاء الجسد عساكره وهو الملك، ومعرفة الله ومشاهدة جمال الحضرة
صفاته

And all the extensions of the body (including the organs) are its troops and it is their king. And understanding of God and witnessing the beauty of his presence is its attribute.[26]

والتكليف عليه، والخطاب معه، وله الثواب، وعليه العقاب، والسعادة والشقاء
تلحقانه، والروح الحيواني في كل شيء تبعه ومعه، ومعرفة حقيقته، ومعرفة صفاته،
مفتاح معرفة الله سبحانه وتعالٰ،

And all the burdens are on it. And the Divine Speech was meant for it. And to it is the reward. And upon it is (also) the punishment. And felicity and damnation follow it. And the Animus spirit is, in everything, subservient to it and is ever with it. And understanding is its reality. And understanding is its quality. It is the key to understanding God, Glorified and Exalted is He.

فعليك بالمجاهدة حتى تعرفه؛ لأنه جوهر عزيز من جنس جوهر
الملائكة، وأصل معدنه من الحضرة الإلهية، من ذلك المكان جاء، وإلى ذلك المكان
يعود

So upon you is the struggle until you come to know it. For it is a precious essence from the genus of the Angelic essence. Its origin is from the Divine Presence. From there does it come. And to that destination will it return.

---

26 Its prime attribute or its fundamental nature. The Heart was created for the sole purpose of recognizing Divinity. If it is sound and healthy, it has no other inclination, and that inclination is a sign of its health. If it demonstrates any other inclination other than an inclination towards divinity, then that becomes symptomatic of it being diseased.

ما حقيقة القلب

What is the reality of the Heart?

فالإنسان من عالم الخلق من جانب، ومن عالم الأمر من جانب

Man is of the Realm of Creation in one aspect, and of the Realm of Intent in another aspect.[27]

فكل شيء يجوز عليه المساحة والمقدار والكيفية فهو من عالم الخلق

And every "thing" that has the possibility of occupying space, can be measured, and has a "how-ness" to it being, is from the Realm of Creation.[28]

وليس للقلب مساحة ولا مقدار، ولهذا لا يقبل القسمة، ولو قبل القسمة لكان من عالم الخلق

But the Heart does not occupy space, nor can it be measured, and as such cannot be divisible, for if it could be divided, it would be from the Realm of Creation.[29]

---

27 The Created Realm, عالم الخلق is the manifest realm. It is where the form, shape, structure, substance, and symbol, is found. This is the outward. This outward manifestation has an inward reality that gives it its reality. This is the Realm of Intent, or Affair, عالم الأمر, where the Command, Order, Intent, Will, Meaning, and Essence is found. Both these dimensions belong to the Almighty by His saying ألا له الخلق والأمر. These two Realms belong to two dominions respectively. The *Mulk* ملك, which is of a material nature. And the *Malakūt* ملكوت, which is of an Ethereal or Spiritual nature. All physical and formal aspects of creation belong to the former. All ontological and teleological aspects belong to the latter. This includes thoughts, emotions, intentions, will, consiousness, and the likes.

28 Meaning if it has spatial dimensions, can be given a unit of measure, be it size, volume, mass, density or any form of measurement, and it has a 'how-ness' to its being, an algorithmic process of creation, it is thus from the realm of form, shape, structure, substance, or symbol. Here, if you ponder on it more deeply, whatever object you analyze, if it fulfills one or all of these conditions, it would be an object with some materiality to it.

29 In other words, the Heart has no physical attributes, because physicality can be measured, can occupy space, can undergo a transformational process, can be divided into smaller and smaller components that make up the whole (atoms and molecules and such)

وكان من جانب الجهل جاهلا ومن جانب العلم عالما، وكل شيء يكون فيه علم وجهل فهو محال

And this would be in a state of ignorance, ignorant, and in a state of knowledge, knowledgeable. And anything that is both ignorant and knowledgeable (at the same time) is an impossibility.[30]

وفي معنى آخر هو من عالم الأمر، لأن عالم الأمر عبارة عن شيء من الأشياء لا يكون للمساحة والتقدير طريق إليه.

In the other meaning (of it) it is from the Realm of Intent. Because the Realm of Intent explains those things that do not occupy space and can be divisible in their modes.[31]

This is your inner reality. This is who you are in your essence. These are the qualities imbibed in you. Not, as Ghazali says, to imprison you. But to set you free. In other words, they were not placed in you that you become their prisoner, by submitting to them. For to submit to them is to succumb to their unguided whims. Your desires, your irascibility, your inclinations of plotting and planning, are your assets if you nurture and regulate them. They are not intellective. They cannot be the drivers of your being, rather you should be driving them. You should control them, not them controlling you.

And there is only one pathway you can follow to ensure your control. The right to rule this dominion of yours as entrusted to you by your Creator. You must ensure that you are in control of your heart. And

---

30 A fundamental principle of logic - A thing cannot be one and its opposite at the same time. The allegory of knowledge and ignorance is simple enough. Once you "know" something, you cannot "un-know" it. You cannot be ignorant of it. The knowledge can be forgotten, but it is never removed. This goes deeper into the essence of knowledge being something that is eternally imprinted into the being. It cannot be removed by anyone or anything, except by the Almighty Himself. In reference to the Heart, it cannot be said to be a physical thing and yet have no physical properties.

31 This then is the Metaphysical explanation, that the Heart is Metaphysical. The Realm of Intent can thus be called the Metaphysical Realm, which explains the ontological nature of things, where the ontology of a thing is "other than" (Meta) physical.

your heart is in control of your intellect. And your intellect is in control of your moods and desires. Lest you succumb to a bestial nature, or a predatory nature, or a demonic nature, and seal your fate as one who is damned to the abyss.

You were created to attain an Angelic Rank, one that is dedicated purely to the Praise and Glorification of God Almighty. Concupiscent, irascible, and demonic natures are not from their attributes.

If you seek contentment, and you find it in any of these categories, then indulge in those inclinations. However, if you find contentment in being Angelic in nature, then seek to rid yourself of all these chains. For the Angelic nature is pure. You must seek purity for the heart. You must humble your 'self' before yourself. You must be sincere in your pursuit. You must reflect on your intentions, your actions, and your speech, and thus evaluate your shortcomings. You must struggle against your 'self,' overpower it, and rise to a lofty degree by submitting your entirety to the Will of God.

That is the true meaning of being a Muslim.

THE EPIC OF MAN

The "Epic" of man is fundamentally the single most important story that mankind can value. There is no tale truer or more relatable than man's origin, what transpires of him through time, and the finality of that tale in proportions unfathomable. No matter what man has conceived of storytelling for eons of his existence, never could he conceptualize what has been ordained by the Master Author Himself in what He, the Most Exalted, has conceived and relayed.

This epic, yet to conclude, beholds secrets deepest in its origin. It defines the very nature of the characters involved, the essence of their being, and the purpose of their creation. It is presented in such a way as to behold suspense in each unfolding moment, unpredictable in its outcomes, so intricately interwoven and sophisticated. But what truly sets this epic on a pedestal of honor is its perfect balance and precise deliverance. Its climax and epilogue defines its debut, and its inauguration defines its structure, integrity, plot, and narrative.

This is what we seek to unravel in this chapter. In knowing your 'self' you must know what preempted your being. You must know what role you were defined to play. You must know the peripheries that dictate how that role is played. In this epic, you must know who the protagonist is and who the antagonist is, and how each one defines the other. You must also learn the bittersweet symphony of this epic by which each character shapes its own outcome, wherein you may become either among the side that stands for the greater good existentially, or among the side that is evil and damned to eternal ruin.

Thus it began with a remarkable declaration. He, the Almighty, said that in this material realm, the lowest of the low, He would thus be placing a worthy governor.

To govern whom? Or what?

وَإِذْ قَالَ رَبُّكَ لِلْمَلَـٰٓئِكَةِ إِنِّى جَاعِلٌ فِى ٱلْأَرْضِ خَلِيفَةً ۖ قَالُوٓاْ أَتَجْعَلُ فِيهَا مَن يُفْسِدُ فِيهَا وَيَسْفِكُ ٱلدِّمَآءَ وَنَحْنُ نُسَبِّحُ بِحَمْدِكَ وَنُقَدِّسُ لَكَ ۖ قَالَ إِنِّىٓ أَعْلَمُ مَا لَا تَعْلَمُونَ

And when your Lord said to the angels, "Indeed, I will place in the material realm a governor. They said, "Will You place therein one who causes corruption therein and sheds blood, while we glorify You with praise and sanctify You? He [Allāh] said, "Indeed, I know that which you do not know."[32]

This *Āyah* alone may suffice the core of our discussion in this chapter. Defined in it are the following elements; the governor, the appointment of the governor, the destination of appointment, the nature of this destination, what will distinguish the governor from what is assumed of him.

The Āyah uses the term خَلِيفَة, which most have translated as "Vicegerent," "Successive Authority," "Ambassador," and other such titles that bear political meanings. We argue, however, that none of these are fitting translations on the simple merit that if Ādam was the first Khalīfah, which Khilāfah did he establish? If he was sent to rule, who in particular did he rule? If he was sent to establish a state, what state did he establish? Then there are those who state that he is God's successive authority, a representative of His sovereignty on earth, to which we argue, *why* does God need a representative when He is the Ruler Supreme? His is Sovereign Eternal. He did not need, does not need, and never will He

---

32 Sūrah Al-Baqarah 2:30

need, someone else to settle His affairs for him.

In this we propose a more spiritual meaning of the word خَلِيفَةٌ. That this is a "governor"... not of others, but of himself. He was created to serve his Lord and to be in His presence, which is nigh impossible if he is in a state unworthy. His mission thus is to make himself worthy by removing from his being that which defines the realm of the lowest of the low.

The angels thus disclose an important element. First أَتَجْعَلُ فِيهَا "will you place therein." This is the destination in question. This particular realm which we perceive in its materiality. Which we ratify from its causes and effects. It is a realm where things can take form and those forms can decay. A realm where good and evil are seemingly equivalent possibilities. So why was this destination chosen? Why not somewhere in the Heavens?

Then they said مَن يُفْسِدُ فِيهَا وَيَسْفِكُ ٱلدِّمَاءَ "who will cause corruption there, and shed blood." This is the nature of this realm. Concupiscence, which culminates into Corruption, and Irascibility, which culminates into Bloodshed. The former is the Bestial Quality we discussed in the previous chapter, and the latter is the predatory quality. Together, the culminate into Demonic Qualities. The contrast is presented as the Angelic Quality, by them saying, وَنَحْنُ نُسَبِّحُ بِحَمْدِكَ وَنُقَدِّسُ لَكَ, "And we glorify You with praise, and sanctify You." In other words, the Angels are in the Divine Presence, wherein the praise and glorification of God is not a mere possibility, but a necessity. It is a presence where the *only* deed is that which praises and glorifies God Almighty. Hence His saying;

$$\text{ٱلْحَمْدُ لِلَّهِ رَبِّ ٱلْعَٰلَمِينَ}$$

All praise is due to Allāh, the Lord of the Worlds[33]

So why not place this creature in that rank, where it would be, by that nature, in this state of glorification? We say that God creates all to be inherently of a pure nature, in that His creation is inherently a praiseworthy creation. Why then would He place this creation, that He Himself has honored, in a realm that can, by its nature, cause this creation to be ruined?

---

33 Sūrah Al-Fātihah 1:2

41

This is what we want to understand. Because the angels are posing a highly intelligent query, which is of an absolute truth. This is the nature of this realm. It is causal-effectual. Unintelligent. Reactive. Volatile. Destructive. Why has God Almighty chosen this as the destination?

He thus responds by saying, إِنِّىٓ أَعْلَمُ مَا لَا تَعْلَمُونَ, *"I know that which you do not,"* meaning I know what I am doing! This creature will be unique. I will grant him that which will aggrandize his uniqueness, with which he will discipline the nature of this realm as he will himself, as will also be in his nature, and thus will he *earn* his place in My presence. This is the Divine Favor granted to man, along with a right to claim that favor.

For within man, He the Almighty placed a unique ability never granted to any other creature before. Language. Which will grant him the means to acquire knowledge. Knowledge that would give him understanding. An ability with which he could cross from the realm of form and symbol, to a realm of meaning, and that meaning would show him what it truly means to understand Divinity.

وَعَلَّمَ ءَادَمَ ٱلْأَسْمَآءَ كُلَّهَا ثُمَّ عَرَضَهُمْ عَلَى ٱلْمَلَٰٓئِكَةِ فَقَالَ أَنۢبِـُٔونِى بِأَسْمَآءِ هَٰٓؤُلَآءِ إِن كُنتُمْ صَٰدِقِينَ

And He inspired Ādam all the names. Then He presented them to the angels and said, "Inform Me of the names of these, if you are truthful." [34]

Note my translation. Most have used the phrase, "He taught Ādam all the names." While such translations can be accurate lexicologically, they are inaccurate contextually, because the projected meaning is often a teaching of sorts, an instructor to a student. The word عَلَّمَ as a verb must be understood in the relative time in which the action was performed. If we say, for example, "he wrote," the particular meaning would differ based on when the action was performed, because the very instruments of writing are different in each era. In the present era, one might picture a ballpoint pen. Three centuries prior, a fountain pen. Before that a feathered quill. Prior to that, reed or bamboo. Even further, a stylus. The same applies to paper, parchment, papyrus, leather, bone, clay. Likewise,

---

34 Sūrah Al-Baqarah 2:31

the mode of "teaching" here, عَلَّمَ, must be understood in the age and environ in which the action was performed. I hope to spend sometime here to elaborate how this term must be understood, for it is not a word that can be given a straight definition in the context of its use.

You must first suspend all preconceived definitions of the word in whatever language it has been translated in. You must do this with the entire Qurān regardless. You must then regard the word as an action, in which case you must also understand the one performing the action, thus asking the questions;

Firstly, does God relate with man in the same manner as man relates with man? If so, then the act of عَلَّمَ can be loosely understood as 'teaching' in whatever contemporary form the teaching is done, which would be an incorrect understanding. Since God is unlike anything of His creation, the action performed also is unlike that which creation would do, hence the term in context, being Almighty Allāh who is doing the act of عَلَّمَ must be suspended of all known mannerisms.

Secondly, when and where was the action performed? If we assume that the action was performed in an earthly dimension, this would be incorrect. For God does not have a material form, nor do His actions, but that their manifestations may take on a material form. Which is to say that the action itself is immaterial, but what results from it can have a material manifestation. The manifestation is in man, who is a material creation, but between him and his Creator, we must suspend all notions of materiality. And the same applies to every other instance of the action عَلَّمَ in relation to Almighty Allāh.

The action itself is a form of stimulating the soul into a mode of visualizing meanings, immaterial and independent of the forms and symbols that represent them. It is what facilitates the 'knowing' with which the act of acquiring knowledge can be facilitate, since knowledge itself is immaterial, and meanings are immaterial, hence 'knowing the meanings' is itself immaterial. The action of عَلَّمَ is also immaterial. Everything that is used as an instrument of performing the action is independent of the action itself which can be performed without the instruments. This is why we emphasize suspending all preconceived notions in the understanding of this word, without which understanding the meaning of ٱلْأَسْمَآء cannot be possible.

43

We say that this is a casting إلقاء into the very essence of man في روعه an ability قوّة by which he can speak intelligibly نطق بها.[35] It was placed in him. What was placed? A list of names? A dictionary of sorts? Where was it placed? On the brain? The tongue?

No... this was language.

Man was given language. Not the Arabic language. Or English. French or Japanese.

Language in essence. That which construes meaning. Meaning that can be articulated. The ability by which phonemes could be built into words. Words that could be associated with forms and objects, by which they could be named, defined, described, elaborated, and thus understood. This is a far more complicated matter to explain, which is why I have dedicated it a separate chapter.

But understand here, that this ability was not granted to any other creature. Indeed, when the challenge was presented to the Angels, and they found themselves unable to perform, it was because they did not *know* what to do or how to do it.

قَالُوا سُبْحَٰنَكَ لَا عِلْمَ لَنَآ إِلَّا مَا عَلَّمْتَنَآ إِنَّكَ أَنتَ ٱلْعَلِيمُ ٱلْحَكِيمُ

They said, "Exalted are You; we have no knowledge except what You have taught us. Indeed, it is You who is the Knowing, the Wise." [36]

It was an attempt made by the Angels to acquire the knowledge of a thing by *naming* the thing. A process we would call "abstraction of essence." Since the physical object cannot be placed *inside* the being, the only way he knows of it is through its formal association with what it means. Man has been granted access to the realm of symbols which allows him to link forms to their essences by understanding what those essences mean, a feat accomplished through the naming of things. It is the name, or symbol, that carries the meaning, or knowledge of the thing to be known, and embedded in that meaning is the thing's essence and its purpose of creation. This process has no materiality to it, no tangibility.

---

35 Al-Rāghib al-Isfahānī, *Al-Mufradāt fī Gharīb al-Qurān*

36 Sūrah Al-Baqarah 2:32

It is purely metaphysical. Or unseen, a matter to which God alone has access to in its knowledge.

قَالَ يَـٰٓأَادَمُ أَنۢبِئۡهُم بِأَسۡمَآئِهِمۡ فَلَمَّآ أَنۢبَأَهُم بِأَسۡمَآئِهِمۡ قَالَ أَلَمۡ أَقُل لَّكُمۡ إِنِّىٓ أَعۡلَمُ غَيۡبَ ٱلسَّمَـٰوَٰتِ وَٱلۡأَرۡضِ وَأَعۡلَمُ مَا تُبۡدُونَ وَمَا كُنتُمۡ تَكۡتُمُونَ

He said, "O Ādam, inform them of their names." And when he had informed them of their names, He said, "Did I not tell you that I know the unseen [aspects] of the heavens and the earth? And I know what you reveal and what you have concealed." [37]

It is thus forked in twain. Knowledge of that which is unseen of the heavens and the earth, granted to man only when God reveals it through His Divine Speech. And that which man knows and comes to know, what he discovers and unravels through his reason and rationality. *Two* streams of knowledge. Not just the one he supposes to exist in his sensoria.

This ability is a Divine Gift. The prime favor bestowed upon man, which if he uses correctly he will successfully navigate the realm of concupiscence and irascibility, and rightfully earn a place in the rank of glorifying God. It is an ability worthy of prostration to.

وَإِذۡ قُلۡنَا لِلۡمَلَـٰٓئِكَةِ ٱسۡجُدُواْ لِءَادَمَ فَسَجَدُوٓاْ إِلَّآ إِبۡلِيسَ أَبَىٰ وَٱسۡتَكۡبَرَ وَكَانَ مِنَ ٱلۡكَـٰفِرِينَ

And [mention] when We said to the angels, "Prostrate before Ādam!" So they prostrated. Except for Iblīs. He refused, and was arrogant, and became of the disbelievers. [38]

Now we will introduce the antagonist of the epic.

One might ask; what was Iblīs's justification? Could it be, if given the benefit of the doubt, something he was unaware of? Something that caused him hesitation, that ultimately lapsed the moment such that he was unable to obey the command? Which is to say that *may be* benefit of doubt he did not understand the Command? Or that the unfolding

---

37 Sūrah Al-Baqarah 2:33

38 Sūrah Al-Baqarah 2:34

of events caught him by surprise? Any number of causes can be used to excuse him, or justify his actions. And yet, this is not the case, for what transpired was concluded to be a matter unforgivable. To be classified as a Kafir is not simply a matter of disbelief. It is that the individual knows the truth, understands the truth, despite which they consciously elect to deny the truth. Ergo, a disobedience in such a state cannot be justified or excused, since the individual was well aware of what was expected of them. The decision to refuse was a conscious one, and is thus regarded as obstinate defiance.

We argue this matter from the Qurān, that this was not a matter abruptly ordained. There was a clear indication that such a matter will come to pass. That Almighty Allāh had already informed them (the Angels and Iblīs included) that He will indeed be creating this unique creature called 'Man' and that when it was complete, they, the occupants of the Heavens were to show their utmost respect by prostrating before Man.

$$\text{فَإِذَا سَوَّيْتُهُ وَنَفَخْتُ فِيهِ مِن رُّوحِى فَقَعُوا لَهُ سَٰجِدِينَ}$$

So when I have proportioned him and breathed into him of My [created] soul, then fall down to him in prostration." [39]

Iblīs did argue, "How am I to prostrate to other than Allāh?"[40] The standard excuse for doing or not doing what is explicitly commanded is typically a manipulation of Fiqh, which we would rightly call "Iblīs's Methodology." The scholars identify two kinds of prostration. The Prostration of Reverence سجود تشريف, as a sign of respect and veneration, which is permissible to the limits and intents that are not worshipful. And the Prostration of Worship سجود عبادة, which is by its definition

---

39 Sūrah Sād 38:72, and Sūrah Al-Hijr 15:29

40 From the famous recounting of Imām Junayd Al-Baghdādi and his meeting with Iblees when he asked the devil, *"O accursed one, what was it that held you back from prostrating to Adam?"* It has been recorded by notable Sufi scholars such as Ali al-Hujwiri in his *Kashf al-Mahjūb*, and Farīd ud-Dīn Attār in his *Tadhkirat al-Awliyā*. Its authenticity of the incident is debatable, but is affirmed to be true by many classical scholars. My mentioning it here is simply for illustrative purposes.

reserved for the Lord Almighty alone.[41] What was commanded to the Angels and Iblīs was of the former kind. Hence his excuse is a blatant and devious lie!

He may have lied to Imām Junayd, or perhaps to whomever else he also met in human history, but one cannot lie in the presence of their Lord. It is inherently an impossibility to do so.[42] Hence when he was asked as such;

$$\text{قَالَ يَٰٓإِبْلِيسُ مَا لَكَ أَلَّا تَكُونَ مَعَ ٱلسَّٰجِدِينَ}$$

He (Allāh) said, "O' Iblis, what is it to you, that not you were you among the Prostrators?"

He replied as such, unable to conceal the truth;

$$\text{قَالَ لَمْ أَكُن لِّأَسْجُدَ لِبَشَرٍ خَلَقْتَهُ مِن صَلْصَٰلٍ مِّنْ حَمَإٍ مَّسْنُونٍ}$$

He (Iblis) said, "Nay would I prostrate to man created of clay from black mud altered."[43]

---

41 You should know that the former, سجود تشريف, has been annulled by Islām, which itself annuls all previous dispensations of faith. When the last and final testament, and its ordainments, were revealed to mankind through the Prophet Muhammad (ﷺ), *all* forms of prostration to other than Allāh had been prohibited. Prior to this, certain dispensations maintained a prostration to others, and this is most common in Hinduism. If examined from a *Fiqh* perspective, at the time of Adam, this form of prostration was permissible, as is evident by Allāh's command. But is impermissible also by Divine Ordinance to perform it anymore. This is where Iblīs's craftiness becomes more apparent. As Imām Junayd was a well-versed scholar of the religion, he knew that by the *Sharī'ah* no one is allowed to prostrate to other than Allāh. But he also knew that the command to prostrate had come from Allāh in an age when the prohibition was not yet in effect. Hence it was concluded that Iblīs was *lying*, because it was not about the *act* of prostration rather it was a matter of disobedience. Iblīs's *Kufr* is thus classified as كفر الإعراض والاستكبار, the *Kufr* of Disobedience (infidelity) and Arrogance.

42 Which is a truly remarkable matter, as it applies to all of creation. One can lie to their fellow, conceal the truth from each other, but this cannot be done before Almighty Allāh. Hence his statement as *"I know the unseen [aspects] of the heavens and the earth, And I know what you reveal and what you have concealed."*

43 Sūrah Al-Hijr 15:32-33

It demonstrates from his own statement that the kind of prostration was not that of worship, and likewise, he was not removed from the awareness that such an act was expected from him. For they were all aware of the kind of prostration that was commanded of them. They, and Iblīs included, knew that this moment would arise. He knew what he was supposed to do, but he did what he *wanted* to do. And in that doing, he established his political position. He was making a statement, and it was duly noted.

$$\text{فَقُلْنَا يَآدَمُ إِنَّ هَذَا عَدُوٌّ لَّكَ وَلِزَوْجِكَ فَلَا يُخْرِجَنَّكُمَا مِنَ الْجَنَّةِ فَتَشْقَىٰ}$$

So We said, "O Ādam, indeed this is an enemy to you and to your wife. Then let him not remove you from Paradise so you would suffer.[44]

Be wary of this fellow. He has an ulterior motive. God intended thus to test man's resolution. Did he truly understand what this matter entailed? More so, for him to navigate the material realm, his ordained destination, he would need guidance. For if he were to follow the devil, he would suffer, hence if he were to follow Allāh he would be saved from the suffering.

But he still needed to be prepared. The moment he would enter the material realm, he would be in engulfed by its nature, where for him to seek the protection of the Divine Presence, he would need to learn to part himself from the nature of this world. And for that, he would need a set of rules and guidelines to follow.

He would need a *Shar'īah*.

But even more constitutive than that, he would need to first understand what is meant by *Shar'īah*. It is not simply a matter of knowing the law. One must understand why he must follow the law, the understanding of which must itself be pure, the purity of which must itself be established and ingrained into the essence of man *before* he has been tainted by the nature of the material realm. Hence the following test is enacted for him.

---

44 Sūrah Ṭāhā 20:117

وَقُلْنَا يَـٰٓـَٔادَمُ ٱسْكُنْ أَنتَ وَزَوْجُكَ ٱلْجَنَّةَ وَكُلَا مِنْهَا رَغَدًا حَيْثُ شِئْتُمَا وَلَا
تَقْرَبَا هَـٰذِهِ ٱلشَّجَرَةَ فَتَكُونَا مِنَ ٱلظَّـٰلِمِينَ

And We said, "O Ādam, dwell, you and your wife, in Paradise, and eat therefrom in [ease and] abundance from wherever you will. But do not approach this tree, lest you be among the wrongdoers." [45]

Do this and this, as this is permissible for you by law. But do not do this and that, as that is prohibited for you. The resultant of the former will hence be regarded as pious and righteous. The resultant of the latter will thus be regarded as evil. Since man is created as a goodly creation, to do that which is ordained by his Creator in that which is permissible for him to do, is itself inherently good and is a fulfillment of his true nature. For him to do other than what is ordained, in transgression or defiance, is contrary to his goodly nature and is hence a capitulation to evil, a capitulation to the nature of this realm, which is its concupiscence and irascibility.

In this regard, he not only needs to know, but to clearly understand what to do and what not to do. He will need *Sharī'ah*. This is what was entasked to him. Permissible it is for you to do such and such and such. But prohibited for you is this other. It was not a matter of the tree or its fruit. It was matter of obedience. Regardless of what benefit it might contain. What pleasure it might bring. What joy or happiness you might gain. Your Lord has forbidden you from it. Will you, O' Believer, obey your Lord regardless of your inclinations? Regardless of your rationale? Will you place Revelation in judgment over reason? Or will you place whim and desire over Revelation and reason?

You must also remember then, that the task is not as simple as stated. There are forces at play whose sole self-appointed mission is to ensure your transgression. They are relentless in their pursuit to alter your perception, inner and outer, by casting doubt upon the certainty of obedience, so that your own volition overpowers your inherent nature,

---

45 Sūrah Al-Baqarah 2:35

49

to corrupt it from its purity into something that is decayed. Like the scorpion who stung the frog, it is in the nature of our antagonist to deceive us. He does not waste a waking moment, and he began the first opportunity he got.

See his chicanery. His sophistry. See how logical and rational an idea he can give. See how twisted his own mind really is. Look at what he is falsely promising. The language he is using. The casuistry with which he is tantalizing, that which seems unattainable. He seems to be telling the truth, and that "truth" is that *your Lord is lying to you!*

As if that could ever be true!

For can God Almighty ever be anything but the Truth?

And yet, look around you, dear reader. What do you see? What do you hear? Grasp the essence of the following Ayah, the Divine Truth from Almighty Allāh, and attest to His Majesty. For the same lie uttered by the devil to Adam is the same lie uttered to you today. He is devious and cunning, but lacks imagination and creativity. It makes him weak. It makes him predictable. Do not let this foolish intellectual gain victory over you!

فَوَسْوَسَ إِلَيْهِ ٱلشَّيْطَٰنُ قَالَ يَٰٓـَٔادَمُ هَلْ أَدُلُّكَ عَلَىٰ شَجَرَةِ ٱلْخُلْدِ وَمُلْكٍ لَّا يَبْلَىٰ

> *So the devil whispered to him; he said, "O Ādam, shall I direct you to the tree of immortality and a kingdom that shall never decay?"* [46]

Man was naive. Innocent. He was still learning, experiencing *Sharīah* for the first time. He was learning, through the experience of his existence, that there are indeed rules and those rules have consequences. But Iblīs had walked this earth for ages before. He was already well-versed in what this reality entailed. And he knew precisely where to press. So he tested the waters.

فَوَسْوَسَ لَهُمَا ٱلشَّيْطَٰنُ لِيُبْدِيَ لَهُمَا مَا وُۥرِيَ عَنْهُمَا مِن سَوْءَٰتِهِمَا وَقَالَ مَا نَهَىٰكُمَا رَبُّكُمَا عَنْ هَٰذِهِ ٱلشَّجَرَةِ إِلَّآ أَن تَكُونَا مَلَكَيْنِ أَوْ تَكُونَا مِنَ ٱلْخَٰلِدِينَ

---

46 Sūrah Tāhā 20:120

But Satan whispered to them to make apparent to them that which was concealed from them of their private parts. He said, "Your Lord did not forbid you this tree except that you become angels or become of the immortal." [47]

His mission was, and always has been, simple. To expose man for his blameworthy qualities. To prove man's unrighteousness. To shame him before his Lord. Man was well aware that he was created to be angelic and to be immortal. This knowledge is embed in his primordial nature. But the promise is not inherent. It has to be hard earned. So what if a quicker more easier path could be navigated? Eat of the tree and live the dream. Seems too good to be true. Unless the devil swears by it.

$$وَقَاسَمَهُمَآ إِنِّى لَكُمَا لَمِنَ ٱلنَّٰصِحِينَ$$

And he swore [by Allāh] to them, "Indeed, I am to you from among the sincere advisors." [48]

Ask him, when he whispers such desires to you, how is it that *you*, of all other people, have the shortcut to success, when the Lord has ordained a different path?

"No," says the devil, "Trust me. I am telling the truth. I am but sympathetic to your cause." His justification is thus; your Lord wants to send you into a realm of toil and hardship. It is a realm in which you will be helpless and powerless, and that will see you to certain death. "Believe me, I know," says he, "I have been there. My people, the Jinn, have suffered the harshness of that world."

$$فَدَلَّىٰهُمَا بِغُرُورٍ ۚ فَلَمَّا ذَاقَا ٱلشَّجَرَةَ بَدَتْ لَهُمَا سَوْءَٰتُهُمَا وَطَفِقَا يَخْصِفَانِ عَلَيْهِمَا مِن وَرَقِ ٱلْجَنَّةِ ۖ وَنَادَىٰهُمَا رَبُّهُمَآ أَلَمْ أَنْهَكُمَا عَن تِلْكُمَا ٱلشَّجَرَةِ وَأَقُل لَّكُمَآ إِنَّ ٱلشَّيْطَٰنَ لَكُمَا عَدُوٌّ مُّبِينٌ$$

---

47 Sūrah Al-A'rāf 7:20

48 Sūrah Al-A'rāf 7:21

So he made them fall, through deception. And when they
tasted of the tree, exposed to them was their shame, and they began
(immediately) to fasten together over themselves from the leaves
of Paradise. And their Lord called to them, "Did I not forbid
you from that tree, and said unto you that indeed the devil is to
you an explicit enemy?" [49]

You should know that a deal with the devil is not signed in blood.
It is a long series of negotiations. Step by step. He cantillates the hymns
most prickling to your curiosity. He instills the melodies most soothing
to your soul. He plays the symphonies most mellifluous to your heart.
He steals your confidence. He embezzles your trust. And at the very
dire moment, at the cusp, he slithers back into the shadows, grinning
as you take your fall.

But this is where the pearl is truly found. At the heart of it all. This
is the moment you realize who you truly are, as you see your flaw, if and
only if you acknowledge your fault. You made a mistake, but it is not
about the mistake, rather it is about what you will do to rectify it. God
was testing man's resilience and endurance, but above it all, He was testing
man's resolution and responsibility. After all, He was placing a governor
in the world. A leader of truth and justice. Mistakes will happen, and
there will be accountability. The governor must prove himself worthy
of governance.

Here is where we witness man's true intelligence, deeply entwined
into the fabric of his primordial nature. His recognition of fault,
his admittance of guilt, and submission to the justice of his Lord's
Sovereignty.

قَالَا رَبَّنَا ظَلَمْنَا أَنفُسَنَا وَإِن لَّمْ تَغْفِرْ لَنَا وَتَرْحَمْنَا لَنَكُونَنَّ مِنَ ٱلْخَسِرِينَ

They said, "Our Lord, we have wronged ourselves, and if
You do not forgive us and have mercy upon us, we will surely be
among the losers." [50]

---

49 Sūrah Al-A'rāf 7:22

50 Sūrah Al-A'rāf 7:23

This was Ādam and Hawā's position. Their logic was sound *and* true. Their sense and rationality pure, such that they were closer to the absolute truth than ever before, and their admittance of fault proved their worth.

ثُمَّ اجْتَبَاهُ رَبُّهُ فَتَابَ عَلَيْهِ وَهَدَىٰ

Then his Lord chose him and turned to him in forgiveness and guided [him].[51]

This was the protagonist of this epic. By placing himself in a state of humility, Ādam proved his Lord right, that here was a creation of His, not only capable of high intellection, but equally capable of recognizing the limits of that intellection. Of recognizing his fault through self reflection, acknowledging his weakness, and making an effort to rectify it. He additionally proved that his heart was sound, because he held firm to the conviction he had in his Lord's justice.

Now Almighty Allāh turns His gaze on our antagonist. Man's case has been resolved. What of you now? What do you have to say of your actions?

قَالَ مَا مَنَعَكَ أَلَّا تَسْجُدَ إِذْ أَمَرْتُكَ ۖ قَالَ أَنَا خَيْرٌ مِّنْهُ خَلَقْتَنِي مِن نَّارٍ
وَخَلَقْتَهُ مِن طِينٍ

He [Allāh] said, "What prevented you from prostrating when I commanded you?" He [Satan] said, "I am better than him. You created me from fire and created him from clay."[52]

Note then the construct of the query. Not "*Why* did you not prostrate?" Rather "*What* prevented you?" What stood in your way and obstructed you from seeing the purity of My ordinance?

This is where we remark at the devil's logic and applaud him, sarcastically and rhetorically. Look at this foolish intellectual presenting

51 Sūrah Ṭāhā 20:122

52 Sūrah Al-A'rāf 7:12

a finely constructed syllogism to justify his foolishness. He says, "Fire is better than clay, and since you created me from fire and him from clay, it suffices to conclude that I am better than him!"

See the simplicity in the devil's logic, and the foolishness with which man has adopted it as his own.

I have wealth and riches, he does not, therefore, I am better than him. I am born of a royal family, he is not, therefore I am better than him. My race is superior, his is not, therefore, I am better than him. My Aqīdah is sound, his is not, therefore, I am better than him. My Madhhab is correct, his is not, therefore, I am better than him. I have a degree, he does not, therefore, I am better than him.

The essence of it is always; "I am me, and he is not like me. He does not know what I know. He does not do things the way I do them. He does not believe the way I believe. He does not have the same view as I have. Therefore... "أَنَا خَيْرٌ مِنْهُ"

It is Me, Myself, and I. I am the best, per my undisputed understanding. So why should I acknowledge *his* rank?

This is the moment in which he crippled himself. For the truth is not based on logic and rationality. It is not based on the arbitrary construct of your mind. The truth is what the *Lord Almighty* says is the truth. Logic and rationality are mere instruments of understanding that facilitate the path to truth. Failure to realize this leads to arrogance, and arrogance is a symptom of a highly volatile disease. In the outward, it presents itself with a facade of boldness. But in the inward, it causes a turbulence that can crumble mountains.

The devil was deeply plagued by this illness. He was locking horns with himself. Why is man chosen to be the *Khalīfah*? Have I not served thee for generations? My race supersedes his by eons. He has not even tasted reality and already he is given rank? This, Iblīs saw as an injustice. But never is there injustice in God's ordainment, and so never was there any injustice save for what injustice he did unto himself. And by his saying "I am better than him," he exposed the disease in his heart— jealousy and envy, which manifested in pride and arrogance.

قَالَ فَٱهْبِطْ مِنْهَا فَمَا يَكُونُ لَكَ أَن تَتَكَبَّرَ فِيهَا فَٱخْرُجْ إِنَّكَ مِنَ ٱلصَّٰغِرِينَ

54

He [Allāh] said, "Descend from it [the Divine Presence], for not is it for you to be arrogant therein. So get out; indeed, you are of the disgrace." [53]

Nay! Sayeth the Lord. You are not better than him. And you have proven that you are not better than him, by your very uttering that you are better than him! The devil was thus destroyed by his own logic.

You cannot be arrogant in the Divine Presence!

What is arrogance then?

It is the 'self' expanded beyond its rank. It is the ego inflated. An ego that is not truly intellective, but is rather guided by its concupiscence and irascibility. They deluded him into thinking that he was right and justified in his motifs. And this, rather than earn him a place in the Divine Presence, saw him thus expelled.

"When man erred, he blamed himself and sought forgiveness. When you erred, you blamed other than yourself, and rather than seek absolution, you sought to destroy him. You are irresponsible. You cannot be a *Khalīfah!*"

But once you take that path, there is no hope for you without guidance, for God only guides His light unto those who are worthy. So rather than rectify himself, Iblīs negotiated in a bit to outsmart.

$$ قَالَ أَنْظِرْنِيَ إِلَىٰ يَوْمِ يُبْعَثُونَ $$

He [Satan] said, "Reprieve me until the Day they are resurrected." [54]

Give me time to prove you wrong.

$$ قَالَ إِنَّكَ مِنَ ٱلْمُنظَرِينَ $$

[Allāh] said, "Indeed, you are of those reprieved." [55]

---

53 Sūrah Al-A'rāf 7:13

54 Sūrah Al-A'rāf 7:14

55 Sūrah Al-A'rāf 7:15

Very well... prove Me wrong.

قَالَ فَبِمَآ أَغْوَيْتَنِى لَأَقْعُدَنَّ لَهُمْ صِرَٰطَكَ ٱلْمُسْتَقِيمَ

*[Satan] said, "Because You have put me in error, I will surely
sit in wait for them [i.e., mankind] on Your straight path.*[56]

Still he blamed the Almighty!

ثُمَّ لَءَاتِيَنَّهُم مِّنۢ بَيْنِ أَيْدِيهِمْ وَمِنْ خَلْفِهِمْ وَعَنْ أَيْمَٰنِهِمْ وَعَن شَمَآئِلِهِمْ ۖ وَلَا تَجِدُ
أَكْثَرَهُمْ شَٰكِرِينَ

*Then I will come to them from before them and from behind
them and on their right and on their left, and You will not find
most of them grateful [to You]."*[57]

From the left, the right, front and back. He did not say 'up' and
'down.'

Why?

Because Revelation and guidance comes from above. And humility
comes from below. So long as man maintains his uprightness, whatever
occurs on the horizontal plane will not deter him from his true purpose.
The moment man abandons uprightness, to concern himself with what
is occurring in the periphery, ergo, concern himself with that which does
not concern him, he will be destroyed.

This is the devil's arena. He concerns himself with other than himself.
He does not care for his own fate. He still believes, or rather is deluded
in his belief, that if he is of fire, the Fire will not burn him. Such an
attribute is worthy of the Fire. Such a quality is not worthy of the Divine
Presence. And anyone who embraces this quality earns a direct expulsion
from the Divine Presence. Do not blame other than yourself if that shall

---

56 Sūrah Al-A'rāf 7:16

57 Sūrah Al-A'rāf 7:17

be your fate, for it is a fate sealed by your own doing.

قَالَ ٱخْرُجْ مِنْهَا مَذْءُومًا مَّدْحُورًا ۖ لَّمَن تَبِعَكَ مِنْهُمْ لَأَمْلَأَنَّ جَهَنَّمَ مِنكُمْ أَجْمَعِينَ

He [Allāh] said, "Depart from it [the Divine Presence], reproached and expelled. Whoever follows you among them - I will surely fill Hell with you, all together." [58]

The final act was now complete. The destination set. The pieces in place. Man and Jinn sent into the earthly realm, one entasked to mislead the other, while the other entasked to be led by God's guidance. One will delude your senses with carnal pleasures, the other will awaken your heart to reality.

قَالَ ٱهْبِطَا مِنْهَا جَمِيعًا ۖ بَعْضُكُمْ لِبَعْضٍ عَدُوٌّ ۖ فَإِمَّا يَأْتِيَنَّكُم مِّنِّي هُدًى فَمَنِ ٱتَّبَعَ هُدَايَ فَلَا يَضِلُّ وَلَا يَشْقَىٰ

He [Allāh] said, "Descend from it [the Divine Presence] some of you unto others enemies [of each other]. And should there come to you guidance from Me, then whoever follows My guidance will neither go astray nor suffer.[59]

Behold, then, the Epic of Man.
Marvel it.
Praise its Divine Authorship.
But more than that, study it. Understand it. Grasp its essence. It is not meant to sooth and caresses your longing for entertainment. It is not a framework in an ideology of escapism, or myth recounted by the fireplace. It is a sophisticated cautionary tale, that you may be aware of who you are and where you have come from. This is the truth of your origin. Not some random event in the cosmos of spontaneity from which spawned an insignificant organism that evolved into an insignificant

---

58 Sūrah Al-A'rāf 7:18

59 Sūrah Ṭāhā 20:123

apelike creature that just happened to speak and intellect.

Embedded here is the grandest of all legends, an epic that began with a battle, endures in battle, and will conclude in battle. Between right and wrong. Good and evil. Light and darkness. To determine who will emerge victor and enlightened, and who will be shamed and scorched in defeat.

Man on one side.

Devil on the other.

There is no winning or losing in war. There is only victory and defeat. Everything in the open battlefield remains to be struggled and fought for. There will be deserters, betrayers, defilers of the Divine Covenant. The reality of your being in this realm is a struggle مجاهدة. Persevere the battlefield and emerge the victor. Or succumb and surrender, and be disgraced with the one already disgraced.

The real test lies in you, the lone soldier on the battlefield. Will your heart be shaken? Will the enemy's cry make you doubt the worth of your cause? Are you among those who deceive, defy, and despair? Or among those who rage, violate, and destroy? Or among those who indulge, salivate, and lust? Or are you Man, honored and praised?

Will you be the worthy *Khalīfah*, whom God created to be in His Divine Presence?

Or will you be the bemoaner, whom God cursed and disgraced from His Presence?

LANGUAGE
AND
REVELATION

Language predates human existence. An absolute truth as the hallmark of human civilization. Language defines thoughts. Thoughts define a world-view. World-view dictates cultivation. Cultivation establishes culture. Culture leads to civility. And civility nurtures the civilization. Language is thus the very cornerstone of human existence, the prime attribute without which humanity cannot be called humanity, the very calling of which demands linguistic expression. Man is defined in the uniqueness of his species as حيوان الناطق, the *speaking* animal. There is nothing about the human being, not his sciences, technologies, governances, politics, societies, absolutely *nothing* that can be expressed without language. Mankind should uphold and revere language on a pedestal above *anything* else he can boast about himself.

He must also realize a deeper reality about language, in that it is much more than the external expression and communication of internal thoughts formulated independently of their verbalization. The literal speech or sound escaping the lips is, albeit vital, a minor constituent of language. In demonstrating the adequacy and appropriateness of such a view of language, attention should be drawn to the ways in which one's native language is intimately entwined with, and related to, one's life in a community. This is true of all peoples and all languages. Greater than that, one must revere the language in which God Almighty has chosen to communicate with him, for nothing in all of creation can challenge the Divine Speech in articulation, eloquence, rationality, and expression of reality.

The relationship between language and culture is complex but directly proportional. A detriment to one is a detriment to another, for the two are intertwined. Genealogy and genetics may indicate what biological origin a people could be, but language directly points to who the people truly are. In that regard, one's religion and culture must be made distinct, and if at all they are to be merged, religion must define the culture, such that the religious language becomes the cultural language. As such, learning a language does not only pertain learning its 'alphabet,' word order, or vocabulary. It involves a deep immersion into the culture of the people who speak and express their thoughts, emotions, ideologies and philosophies in that language. The same is true of Scripture. With direct proportionality, embedding oneself in the language of Scripture defines and refines one's culture by refining and defining their worldview.

Being the Speech of Allāh, the language of Scripture is the foundational guide for the human being. It serves as the absolute truth, the criterion by which all other truths are tested for validity. One can truly gauge the intellective capacity of a person based on what they say and how they speak, and Muslims are distinguished by the manner in which they uphold the Speech of Allāh, which reveals the truth of all things, above or below the rationale of worldly scientia.

If one assumes a stance of explaining reality as a derived particular from the universality of the Qurān, then we know they are intellecting. However, if one assumes a stance of explaining reality using science first and *then* attempt to source an Āyah from the Qurān to "prove" it, then we know that such a person is poorly intellecting, if at all. They are deluded into thinking they have discovered a truth of the Qurān, but really they are only trying to 'make things fit.' Because on the one hand they cannot refute the 'empirical proof' of the science, and on the other hand they do not want to sever the emotional link with their religion.

Caught between a rock and a hard place, this results in a desperate bid to find some harmony lest the religion be proven false.[60] And more often than not, they will find some linguistic translative from the Qurān where the scientific expression somehow seems similar to the Qurānic expression.[61] The implication of such epistemologies is the adapted language shapes a word-view in which the Qurān is now affirmed to be the truth since the science has come to some factual truth regarding the same observed entity, as opposed to validating the subjective truth of science using the absolute truth of the Qurān. The flaw in this is that the Qurān is not speaking from an observational perspective. It is not expressing the whatness of reality, since it is not an observational and experimental instrument. The Qurān is expressing the *reality* of reality. Science on the other hand is purely an observational and experimental instrument, and it cannot progress further than the whatness of reality. Which is to say it cannot express the *reality* of reality. It can only express what the observation yields as *realistic.* Both the languages of the Qurān and science are distinct entities. Science deals with a factual reality, a واقعية, that which is *realistic.* The Qurān speaks of reality itself, a حقيقة, that which is *real.*

The Qurān beholds the absolute truth irrefutable because its centrality is on the universal unity of God Almighty, and its meanings are specific, precise, and entirely universal. It does not deal particulars, semantics, or trivial information. Each word has a precise placement, and no word is synonymic to another. Each particle is accounted for and has a purpose to serve, even if it could be grammatically edited or rephrased. Even repetitive statements have their placement in meaning.

The centrality of this *Tawhīd* is not limited to "worshipful acts" only, and this is a major defect in every devout Muslim, Christian, and Jew, to regard religion as a partitive entity whereby everything else is cultivated around it but from it and never blended with it. The centrality

---

60 And such is the apparent case with Christendom's endless struggle with Science, and arguably the core reason attributed to apostasy in Christianity.

61 In this what they are doing is a form of 'Reverse Translation.' You will hear phrases like *"who could have told the prophet this 1400 years ago?"* or *"the Qurān is talking about the 'Big Bang'"* or *"science has discovered what the Qurān said so long ago"* and numerous other phantasmal slogans.

of *Tawhīd* is integral in *all* aspects of life, high or low, worshipful or otherwise, and this includes knowledge. Its language then is the prime determinant of the being's outlook of reality.

Understand then the deep purpose of seeking knowledge in a language of purity. It is not to quantify how much is known. It is to qualify *what* is known. The quantifiable 'how much' pertains the particularities and semantics, as the leaves and branches of a tree, but really the objective is to understand the innermost aspect of the tree where everything converges. Seeking knowledge, rightfully, is a motion from particulars and semantics, to universals, which themselves must be universalized so as to arrive at the ultimate universal knowledge, which is the knowledge of God. For He is indeed the most worthy of knowing.

The centrality of the Qurān is thus to enable this journey, such that through the knowing of God's creation, one can arrive at knowing God. And this is embedded in the very *opening* of the Qurān;

$$ اَلْحَمْدُ لِلَّهِ رَبِّ الْعَٰلَمِينَ $$

All praise is due to Allāh, the Lord of the Worlds[62]

The word عالم is known as an اسم آلة. It is a noun of instrumentation. In other words, it is a 'thing' that facilitates the function of another thing. As an example, مفتاح 'Key', is that which facilitates فتح 'opening'. However the key is not the opening itself. Likewise, the عالم facilitates the علم, or the 'world' facilitates the 'knowledge' or the 'science'. The science does not facilitate the world, nor is the science the world itself. The world exists regardless of the existence of the science. Likewise, 'knowledge' and 'knowing' are not the same. The science is thus the 'key' and what it facilitates is the *knowing* which is the 'opening' to the Knowledge.

By knowing the worlds one can arrive at knowing the Lord of the Worlds, but only if the epistemology is correct. Knowing the Lord of the Worlds, enables the knower to recognize unto whom all praise is due. This is the Angelic rank;

$$ وَنَحْنُ نُسَبِّحُ بِحَمْدِكَ وَنُقَدِّسُ لَكَ $$

And we Glorify You with Praise, and Sanctify You. [63]

---

62 Sūrah Al-Fātihah 1:2

63 Sūrah Al-Baqarah 2:30

Because once you know Allāh, there is nothing else worthy of knowing, and thus nothing else worthy of praise. You can come to know a tree, in all its beauty and marvel, its sheer size, its deep roots, its majestic stature, and you will surely praise it. What then, when you come to know He who created that tree? Would you not disregard the tree entirely?

This kind of knowing is done by the heart. It is not a knowing of rationality, reason, argumentation, or logic, for it is not done by the senses, the brain, or the mind. It is a knowing so deep in the innermost dimensions of the spiritual heart, that it can never be removed. It is a knowing we call *Mushāhadah* مشاهدة, pure witnessing of the Divine Presence. And it rests on the *'Word'* of the Almighty.

He thus sends a message to all, and in particular those who have neglected this word;

قُلْ يَٰأَهْلَ ٱلْكِتَٰبِ تَعَالَوْاْ إِلَىٰ كَلِمَةٍ سَوَآءٍ بَيْنَنَا وَبَيْنَكُمْ أَلَّا نَعْبُدَ إِلَّا ٱللَّهَ وَلَا نُشْرِكَ بِهِۦ شَيْـًٔا وَلَا يَتَّخِذَ بَعْضُنَا بَعْضًا أَرْبَابًا مِّن دُونِ ٱللَّهِ ۚ فَإِن تَوَلَّوْاْ فَقُولُواْ ٱشْهَدُواْ بِأَنَّا مُسْلِمُونَ

Say [to them], "O' People of the Book, come to the Word that is in equity between us and you, that not do we serve and worship except Allāh, and not do we associate with Him anything, nor take each other as Lords other than Allāh." So if they [thereafter] turn away, then say, "Bear witness that we have submitted (to His Will as Muslims)" [64]

That one must not take other than God Almighty as a source of truth and knowledge, for none is equal to Him in rank. He alone is the source of all Knowledge, as He is the Light of the Heavens and the Material World. And if at all they should mock you for this, if they should turn away in obstinate denial, then adhere to your submission to Allāh.

This *'Word'* of equity is in equilibrium across the human race. Each individual not only has access to this 'Word', it is a human right divinely given. This right is the right of the *'Khalīfah'* whom He has ordained to occupy the material domain. I would love to engage you deeper into

---

64 Sūrah Āli 'Imrān 3:64

this subject, but it is not the prime of our discussion here. I only sought to introduce the concept of Language, and all language begins with the 'Word.'

It should suffice then, for the Muslim, if he understands the Arabic of the Qurān, to draw out basic abstract of meaning. It should also suffice the Muslim who does not know Arabic, to look at a sufficiently sound translation and perhaps grasp something of the Qurān's meanings. But the intellect, by nature, is a curious creation. It is ever seeking, and in this search, where the Heart has recognized the Qurān to be the only source of Truth it can cling to, the intellect will attempt to probe further. This probing will result in a 'wondering.'

All philosophy,[65] thus, begins at wonder, and no place else. It is the source intent of seeking truth and wisdom. Its path is that of knowledge,

---

65 There are those who argue that "Philosophy is Harām," and their argument is based on the false premise that philosophy originated *only* from the Greeks. As if to say that no other civilization prior, after, or contemporary to the Greek civilization did not attempt an inquiry into existence and its mysteries. They propagate the idea that philosophy is bad, harmful and should not be pursued on penalty of 'deviancy' and blasphemy. We agree with them on this particular, that their definition of 'Philosophy' is the subject of philosophy, and as with any subject there are facts and theories that are subject to truths and falsities. But to argue that the act of philosophizing is itself "bad" is a fallacious argument, likened to saying that human nature is bad. To philosophize is human nature, and human nature must be refined, likewise, the act of philosophizing must also be refined. To consume anything without cleansing it, or to consume it in excess, is harmful. Any substance with medicinal agency is also a poison. Does medicine inherently become "Harām?" If the study of biology leads to genetic alteration, should not biology also be forbidden? If studying medicine can lead to cosmetic surgery and abortions, or accountancy leading to interest-based financing, should these also not be impermissible? What is the threshold? Where and who determines the line between what is then permissible or forbidden of these? Those who propagate this position regarding philosophy should at the very least recognize the fallacies of their arguments. But to reason with them is akin to reasoning with a stubborn child. They tend to fail miserably, particularly in grasping the modular state of the world which is in effect a manifestation of philosophies, and thus fall into the danger of ignorantly adapting such estranged philosophies like fools enticed by snake oil as medicine. Philosophy is inescapable, whether one does it or it is done for them, and it would behoove them to recognize that an opposition to philosophy is itself a philosophy. To throw out the baby with the bathwater is poor intellection.

and no other. Anything other than that may be arbitrarily termed as 'philosophy' but it is not.[66] Wonder is where the journey begins, and wisdom is its destination. Any who attempts to philosophize without knowledge is but blindly firing an arrow with the hopes of striking the target. This 'wondering' whether assumptive or speculative, is a construct of notions and ideas that must be grounded in something of a truth to endure the test of time. The construct itself cannot be possible without the necessary mediums or components, which we say are construed of language.

Man by his very nature philosophizes, and language lies at the bedrock of all philosophy. Thoughts are formulated, the formulation of which utilizes forms, and the forms themselves cannot occupy spiritual space (in the mind). What exists in the mind is a form conceptualized, the concept of which is abstracted from the forms existent in reality, and the abstraction is a twofold act of association. In one aspect, it is an association of symbol with what the symbol represents. This is outward act from the mind to the physical world. In the other aspect, it is an association of symbol with what the symbol means. This is an inward act from the mind into the essential world.

The mind, which hence exists in this interim between two realms, like the 'horizon' we defined in the second chapter, plays the role of recognizing symbol representing form, and associating that symbol with its meaning.[67] The symbol, then, is a component of language. This is what we want to emphasize in this chapter. Language is the medium by which the being can comprehend reality.

It is the prime quality imbibed into man's nature by which words and

---

66 What I mean by this is that philosophy itself is a human concoction of ideas and notions that attempt to probe the truth to discern its wisdom. If philosophy is not harmoniously sound with Revelation, it remains a set of human ideas and notions, and is subject to rejection. Philosophy does not replace doctrine nor does it become a criterion for judging Revelation. Its validity lies in the philosopher's ability to make the distinction, and its danger lies in an inability to recognize its limits.

67 Understand here that the 'form' exists in the realm of the senses, and the 'meaning' exists in the realm of the heart. The two are not interchangeable. Form cannot exist in the Heart, and meaning cannot exist in the sensorial world. There must be an intermediary responsible for harmonizing the two. This is done by the Intellect.

their articulations are realized. This is rendered by the Almighty's saying, وَعَلَّمَ ءَادَمَ ٱلْأَسْمَآءَ كُلَّهَا *"And He inspired Âdam all the names,"* meaning all the phonemes that lie at the foundation of language construct, through which sophisticated expressions can be built, are all imprinted in the human being. Further to this He says, خَلَقَ ٱلْإِنسَـٰنَ عَلَّمَهُ ٱلْبَيَانَ *"He created man. He inspired (man) with articulation."*

Modernity presents the argument that "science is the hallmark of human civilization" by which they mean that the supposed "civility" of being able to concoct complex mechanisms of entraining the human being with material reality is chiefly reliant on how sophisticated the scientific interpretive can become. In other words, modernity's yardstick of measuring civility is correlated to modernity's technological advancement, both of which are attributed to "science."

We argue the contrary. Language remains the only true hallmark of human civilization, and scientia, whatever derivative it may take, is but a sub-language specific to what the scientia infers. Each science is a container of terms and definitions, observable principles and laws, all structured and organized in a fashion that articulates, logically and rationally, what the science studies. In contrast, the same object of study can be articulated in poetic prose as opposed to linear equations, or colorful art on canvas as opposed to geometric diagrams on paper. It does not matter what the faculty is, the object itself does not change in reality. Only the faculty used to describe it changes. Mathematics, for instance, is a language construed of numbers, all of which are used to articulate the quantitativeness of reality. Physics, likewise, is a language construed of laws used to articulate the physical processes of reality. The same is true of *any* given science. They are all languages in their respective fields.

The language of articulation does not alter that which is being articulated. The only thing altered is its truth or falsehood, regardless of which the thing remains what it is. Its *'it-ness'* provides one with 'knowledge of it' by which one realizes its place in creation. Knowledge of a thing is thus defined simply as *'knowing the proper place of each thing in creation in relation to itself, in relation to everything else, and its relation with the Creator.'* In this regard, one comes to understand that since such relationships exists, there must a medium through which these relationships are cultivated in their perpetual modes of existence.

What we mean by this is that each thing *communicates* with every other thing, and likewise communicates with its Creator. That medium is language. It may not take on the semantic form accustomed to man, may not be executed with the same vocation, may not even have the same logic, but it exists nonetheless. Language is a permeating dimension in all of creation. Every object in creation is *saying* something, some of which is heard and recognized by man, much of which is lost, because man's sensoria has a limitation. They are veiled. And there are also some, like the Prophet-King Sulaymān (ﷺ), whose veils are removed, their limitations expanded, to enable a wider scope of comprehending these oft-overlooked languages of the world.

What is the believer's position then?

It is to be selfless, not selfish, in his perception of reality. It is to understand that there is a living, breathing, speaking reality existent around him, and not to project an egocentric world-view in which he only supposes himself to be of importance. Truly, if one could hear the speech of the trees, not a single one would be cut down. Or the cries of the animals, not a single one would be slain. Mercy takes precedence over rationality. The heart must be sound enough to exercise love and affection for Almighty Allāh's creation, whether or not it can rationalize the significance or insignificance of it.

True intelligence, one that has transcended rationality to comprehending spiritual reality, recognizes that language in the form of words and numbers, sounds and sentences, only construes a meager sapling in a vast forest of 'Language.' That it is not simply a matter of learning the words of a particular semantic form of a language and concluding the matter as having "mastered language." There is a realm beyond that, of meaning and essence, that which enables the existence of language. Without meaning, uttered words have no purpose. The sound is just sound. Pointless. Useless. It is the meaning, and the essence attributed to meaning, that gives words and sentences purpose.

Words are simply formal constructs, symbols that represent what is to be communicated, a collective *medium* of language, not language itself. Words can be replaced by other words, by shapes and symbols, or images, or gestures, even objects, and we find that language can still be applied in communication. A foreigner who does not speak English can communicate his hunger without having to say 'I am hungry.' His expression may take on the form of gesturing to his stomach and mouth, pointing at a restaurant, or even the sound of his grumbling stomach. It does not matter what semantic form he uses, English, Arabic, Chinese, or Russian. It matters what he *means* by saying it.

This is what I intend on showing you here. That there is a 'semantic *form*' that a language takes, which we may call Arabic or English or whatever. Then there is an 'essential *meaning*' to language, which has no form. The former deals with information, much like all the words you see in these pages. The latter deals with knowledge, and in this example, what am I conveying to you? What do I mean?

The two are related, but not equatable. As a simple example, you can master the English language, but not understand anything I am saying. As a more profound example, you can master the Arabic language, but not understand anything of the Qurān.

Why?

Because the semantic form of a language, which is a construct of shapes and symbols, pertain the sensorial faculty. The brain can be programmed to recognize the symbols and their sounds, it can be programmed to piece the information received into rational patterns, but all that does not benefit the being until intellection takes place. You could be looking at the text, reading it even, as most are proficient in *reading* or 'reciting' the Qurān, but haven't an inkling as to what they are reciting. Here you must understand that comprehension does not take place in the brain, which is a component of the body and sensorial world, nor in the intellect, which is a component of the soul and ethereal world. Rather, the comprehension, the realization, the *understanding* takes place in the Heart when the intellect, which is subservient to it, successfully links the perceived symbols to what they mean. Such that even when the symbols themselves are removed from the being's physical presence, their meanings are retained.

What is the relevance of this matter?

This physical material world, or *universe* as we have come to term it, is an '*enclosed entity*.' It cannot explain itself. You can study physicality till kingdom come, you will never unravel its true mystery, its *reality*. For it is, by definition, *not real*. It is only *realistic*. And what I mean by this

68

is that what you perceive as the outward form of everything, whatever your senses pick up in sight, or sound, or taste, or smell, or feel, is only a representation of what it *really* is. And it, by its own rationale, cannot explain what it *really* is. *That* explanation can only come from an external source. A source *outside* the closed-loop. A source of pure and untainted truth. A source that beholds itself as that which originated the realm. God Almighty. Only when He says what it *really* is, can we know its reality. His speech, therefore, is the second-most precious entity after Him. His speech, however, has no physical form. For it is from Him, and He is not a physical entity. His speech, therefore, when it enters into this realm, takes on a preexisting form. One that has enough of a capacity to bear the essence of that speech. One that is itself comprehensible to mankind at a degree of higher intellection, whose symbols touch reality at the very essence. Such a language is not only *chosen* by Him, it is molded and refined by Him, through ages and eons of its conception until such a time as it is ripe for the undertaking.

This is the Arabic Language.

It is arguable that the most profound of all occurrences in human history is the Revelation of the Holy Qurān. What it contains transcends space and time, and its meanings hold true regardless of phenomenal circumstances. It arrived at a time when the language chosen to bear the Speech of God had reached its peak maturity. This 'reaching' could be appreciated as a process of human intellection linked with the language's continual development over the duration of human history from the time of Nabī Ādam (عليه السلام) the first man and prophet, to the time of Nabī Muhammad (ﷺ). Linguists who only examine the semantic form of the language will argue that "Arabic" originated from periods of early antiquity, morphed and shaped by the migrations of proto-semetic and afro-asiatic peoples, all originating from randoms sounds and primitive utterances and gestures. This, they conclude, is based on analyzing the earliest *written* forms of the language. We, however, argue that the language, based on its inherent inflectious properties of root derivations and symbolic meanings, which are themselves deeply embedded in the phonetics of the language, can be traced to articulations by Ādam. Words such as *'ardh'* أرض, *'adan'* عدن , *'Fātir'* فاطر, and many others can be traced to root origins in expressions of reality even before

69

man's descent into the earthly domain, and these are expressed by the Holy Qurān in its articulations of events that foremost occurred before humanity and occurred outside the earthly realm.

It is Divine Ordinance that the descent of the Qurān is timed perfectly to the Holy Prophet's (ﷺ) receiving of revelation, and there is no era past that mark that can ascend to the level of linguistic mastery as *that* moment of revelation. The Holy Qurān introduced concepts that were, and some still are, not known to the civilized world. It presents itself as the *only* explainer of the concepts it introduces, which is to say that not only does it introduce the concepts, it holds them as absolute truth, and it explains them with sophisticated reason and rationality that remain, and will remain, irrefutable. It further proves to the fact of existing concepts that what we *think* we know of them, isn't so. One may look up dictionary or lexicological definitions or explanations of such concepts, but the Qurān will always override whatever we may project. This makes the Qurān's vocabulary to be of the highest intellective order, so much so that it may appear naive and simplistic at first glance, but the deeper one investigates its meanings, more complex and sophisticated understandings are unveiled, because its language, quite literally, carries one from a realm of material expression into realms above and beyond.

To understand His Speech, therefore, you *must* master the Arabic language. Mastering the Arabic language increases intellection, increases inflection, expands ones understanding of reality in a fluid-like manner as opposed to a rigid and purely analytical manner, because reality itself is not only quantitative. It is not rigid. It is not fixed in space and time. It is ever changing. Morphing. One's understanding must be flexible to that change, which can only be possible if the language of articulation has as its inherent property an inflectious nature. For this reason, unlike numerous other writs in history, the Qurān continually proves itself a timeless inscription. It can be analyzed and applied universally to whatever particular in whatever circumstance in whatever age.

What is the additional benefit? We say that the Speech of God is of the highest intelligence. An intelligence so incredibly vast and immeasurable, that all of human capacity collectively can barely scrape the surface. Consider then a sole individual, *you,* who only knows one language, *English*, attempting to understand God Almighty's speech.

Learning a new language is proven to increase intelligence. Every language has its unique collection of symbols and signs (words) and how they come together. The number of sentence-structures formed across all the languages of the world are unquantifiable. In a single language you may describe an object, but in an additional language, the same object can be described differently. This unveils a different perspective. And the more perspectives you have, the more objective your understanding. And the more objective your understanding, the closer you are to Absolute Truth.

Intelligence is the Intellect's ability to intellect. How well the mind can use the tools at its disposal, the senses and the brain, to associate form with symbol and symbol with meaning. The brain itself, a construct of gray-matter and neurons, functions in an algorithmic manner. It is not binary as most assume. Algorithms can be written and rewritten as learning continues. The same neurons can map out multiple algorithms in the same instance. The mapping of algorithms, through learning, is done through language.

If I say, in English, 'Zaid hit Amr,' that sentence can only be spoken in that order. The English language does not allow alternatives like 'Hit Zaid Amr' or 'Amr Zaid hit' or even 'Amr hit Zaid.' This latter sentence is saying something else entirely, and the former sentences are all incorrect. The word order in the English language is fixed. The algorithms generated by the English language are also fixed. These algorithms are incredibly linear and analytical. This may seem trivial, but it has profound effects on one's perception of reality, where space and time are thus perceived as linear, uni-directional, analytical, and purely quantitative.

As a contrast, in Arabic, I can say, زيد ضرب عمرا or ضرب زيد عمرا or زيد عمرا ضرب and all three sentences, are equally correct. Why should there be such a variety? Why not have a single 'correct' way of saying it? Again, it might seem trivial, but it has profound effects. The language thus allows for different ways to articulate the same reality, and the algorithms generated by the language are flexible. They allow for synthetic and non-linear constructs, which allow for broader eruditions of reality, where space and time are perceived as non-linear, multidirectional, synthetic, and both quantitative as well as qualitative.

71

With more languages learned, not only does the brain generate more neural pathways, but the algorithms built along these pathways become more and more sophisticated. This allows the intellect to expand its intellective abilities, by accessing more symbols and thus more meanings, thereby granting the heart greater understanding. People who speak and comprehend different languages think differently. The thoughts they generate in multiple languages are not partitioned from each other, rather they are superimposed, which broadens their scope of thinking. The larger the scope of thought, the better the ability to think critically, deeper, and objectively.

As we have discussed, thinking cannot be done without language. Thinking and dreaming in a particular language shapes the thinker and dreamer's perception of reality. Thoughts are constructs of an inner language. This inner language influences perception in the outward sense as well as decision making in the inward even on subsistent levels, which have higher level consequences. What you say, how you say it, why you say it, all have effects on the outcome of what you will become.

More so, the language you entrain your mind in, will define who you become. If your language is dictated by pop-culture, music, film and entertainment, social media, the kind of language that is deficient, an admixture of what is spoken on the streets and something you read in text books published by the godless world, then your entire perception of reality will be dictated by *them*.

If, on the other hand, your mind is entrained by the Qurānic language, the language of the Prophets, the Companions, the Saints, and the righteous, the language of religion, of high intellection, civility, and discipline, your world-view will be defined accordingly. You will see and comprehend reality as God intended for you. The language of religion disciplines your intellection, which in turn disciplines your 'self'. Likewise, the language of the Qurān, which is God revealing reality to you in His speech, will define your thoughts to be in synchronicity with reality as He has created it.

The choice is yours…

THE BEING
AND EXISTENCE

Every epic needs a conclusion, which itself must be of epic proportions. To have a thing originate in majesty and end in a whimper is untenable to its purpose of being. The culmination of its being must be as significant, if not more, as its origination. This is its *eskhatos*, where all that it was meant to be culminates to the finality of its epic.

The study of this is Eschatology, and the nature of this study is inherently, for mankind, a kind of comprehension of what *will be*. It cannot be studied after its occurrence, for it being the finality of mankind, serves no purpose in being studied *after* human history has ended. It is therefore contingent on factors that are indicative of the End, *Signs* of what is to come, of which many consume to the degree of quenching the thirst of knowing the entirety of human destiny before it has occurred. This is classified as a phantasmal study. Rather they should be studied to the degree of navigating an obscure future. For without a sign on the road, life becomes difficult to journey.

It is not a simple study. Those who delve into it blindly, unequipped with the acumen and requisite knowledges, are parted into two camps. There are those who make extraneous errors that plunge them into confounded states. Then there are those who are drawn into it by its intriguing perplexities and suspense, and are thus enticed by the manner in which it engages their minds, and as a result they seldom grasp the essential purpose of study. Both these camps tend to develop flawed epistemologies that result in their assumptions that the study of Eschatology *only* involves analyzing trending political events paired with prophecies to determine patterns that would lead to certain possible outcomes linked to those prophecies, from which they hence assume to have understood the *Signs* in ways that no one ever has. Rather they assume to have knowledge that no one has, and this leads them to the fancy that they have a gift, or have been chosen to be enlightened.

They are gravely deluded in the matter!

Deluded because they never realize that they are analyzing semantics that keep shifting, facts that keep changing, and more often than not, they are overcome with frustration. Because they cannot understand. Because the heart was never designed to comprehend semantics and particulars. They will often resort to estranged conspiracy theories to 'fill in' the gaps of their flawed epistemologies, much of which are farfetched to extremes of fiction and fantasy.

Eschatology is a field of study that examines the culmination of a continuum, and if it has an ending, it must also have a beginning. Thus, eschatology is truly about studying the entirety of the matter, from the beginning to its end, and what originates the beginning and what is entailed after. For one to succeed in this field, they must examine human history holistically, and observe its transformation, and what one finds is that there is an incredible paradigm shift in human thought from what could be termed as a '*Fitrah*-based' thinking to a '*Dunya*-centric' thinking.

When man was first created, he existed in a realm other than the earthly realm. There are some who would argue that the '*Jannah*' in which Ādam and Hawā were allowed to live was a '*Jannah*' on earth, but they are wrong. This is evident from the Angels' statement أَتَجْعَلُ فِيهَا "will you place *therein?*" If the placement is *therein* فِيهَا, and Ādam and Hawā were expelled from '*Jannah*' to the '*Ardh*' only after they had disobeyed, then what they claim cannot possibly be true.

Nevertheless, that is not our argument here. The point I want to draw your attention to is the 'state' in which they were before they entered this realm. A realm of causes and effects, of happenings and occurrences, a realm in which there are 'Necessaries,' 'Possibilities,' and 'Impossibilites' alike. A realm in which the consciousness residing in the heart can affirm or negate facts but is equally likely to be deceived by those same facts. It is to recognize that the state in which they existed *prior* to entering a realm which would delude their awareness was a state of pure *Fitrah* فطرة.

Fitrah is the primordial nature, an essential intelligence and awareness that is untainted. That is so pure as to recognize and witness the Divine Presence. This is the nature with which man entered into this realm. But he also encountered something else in this realm. That he could craft. Manufacture. Develop. Cultivate. And every progress in development and cultivation prompted a necessity of tools and instrumentations, which he crafted. The Greeks called this type of crafting *Tekhne,* and it served as the root origin of the term *Technology.* In Arabic this is called *Tiqniyyah* تقنية.

Witness then how mankind has changed. He existed in this world chiefly reliant on his own acumen, intellection, his God-given ability, coupled with the guidance God sent down. But his diseased heart saw him striving for the very thing the devil sought to deceive him with. The tree of immorality and a kingdom that never decays. For which he crafted more. And all his pursuit of knowledge is now bent and focused on his *Tiqniyyah*, which is of an outward material reality, as opposed to his *Fitrah*, which is of an inward spiritual reality. All to the attainment of an engineered *Jannah* in this material realm called *Dunya*.

Have you ever wondered whether this pursuit of the modern man serves any existential purpose? This estranged notion where 'success' is defined as having the ability to accumulate an infinite amount of things. When does it end? Where do the limits lay? And what happens when it is all depleted? How much can man truly consume until he affirms existential satisfaction and contentment?

Man's very nature, which once was free and allowed to incline to its disposition, is now suppressed and denied its inherent freedom. Because we have forgotten *who* we are. Where we have come from. Why we are here. And where we are going. We have alienated ourselves from the very thought of our existence. Our *being*.

75

Consider this parable; There were two young fish swimming merrily. They came across a much older fish who asked them, "How is the water?" They swam away without responding. A little further ahead, one of the younger fish asked his companion, *"What is water?"* [68]

You are that younger fish. You are existent. You are a being in existence. But you are oblivious of both your *being* and that which you are existent in. I want you to ponder this deeply. The goal of this chapter is to enable you to understand what that 'water' is.

Know then, that there are three primary things that humankind cannot comprehend. These three, among many others, can never be given a rational explanation. Allow me to reiterate this— there is no scientist, no philosopher, *no one,* regardless of how many academic achievements they have, *no one* can explain these three in a language of scientia. They can be conceptualized, which is to say we know of them in concept, but they cannot be comprehended.

These are: Infinity, Eternity, and Non-Existence. We cannot comprehend infinity, because we are in a finite state of existence. We cannot comprehend eternity, because we are in a temporal state of existence. We cannot comprehend non-existence, because we are in an existent state of existence.

The first is not a subject of discussion in this book. The second will be discussed in chapter 8. The third is what I want you to focus on here.

Being and Existence. This is the most complex concept to grasp, so take your time with it. You are the Being. You are existent.

You must first understand what is meant by 'Existence,' 'Non-existence,' 'Thing,' 'Nothing,' 'Something,' and 'Someone'. You must learn to distinguish these terms for you to arrive at their true and specific meanings. 'Existence' and 'Thing' are not synonymic. Neither is 'Non-existence' and 'Nothing.' Additionally, 'Thing' and 'Something' are not the same thing, and 'Something' and 'Someone' are not alike.

In that regard, you must understand our use of language here. English is deficient in such matters of an existential nature. Which is why this chapter will perhaps be the longest of the lot, as the following pages

---

68 Paraphrased from a commencement speech delivered by David Foster Wallace in 2005 at Kenyon College, Ohio, later published as an essay under the title *"This is Water"* p.2009

will be filled with articulations of these terms beyond their dictionary definitions. I will also implore you to take the Arabic terminology in higher regard than the English translations of them, and only use the English as tertiary 'explanations.'

Let us begin with 'Existence.' The term used in Arabic is وُجُود, from the root word وجد, which bears the meanings of وَجَدَ 'to exist' or 'to be.' If something 'is' then it is regarded as وجد, meaning it is existent. Here, the term bears the highest attribution to God Almighty as اَلْوَاجِدُ, meaning, if at all existence is to be comprehended, it can only be consciously realized, and the highest of conscious realization is اَلْوَاجِدُ, 'The Existent.' Another derivation of the word is وَجَدَ, which means 'to find' or 'to discover,' and if there is an act of 'finding' there must be one which is the 'finder' and that which is 'found.' Whosoever or whatsoever the being seeks, in his finding, he will ultimately only find the One who is truly existent. Hence the Almighty's saying;

$$\text{لَمْ يَجِدْهُ شَيْئًا وَوَجَدَ ٱللَّهَ عِندَهُ}$$

...not does he find a thing, but finds Allāh with him...

In other words, perception itself is a proponent of existence. The being is perpetually looking, seeing, observing, and witnessing, all for the sake of seeking the One. This is done whether the being is a believer in the One, or otherwise. The only difference is that the former knows what he is looking for, and the latter is veiled. He falls in the context of the Ayah above, elaborated fully as;

$$\text{وَٱلَّذِينَ كَفَرُوٓا۟ أَعْمَٰلُهُمْ كَسَرَابٍۭ بِقِيعَةٍ يَحْسَبُهُ ٱلظَّمْـَٔانُ مَآءً حَتَّىٰٓ إِذَا جَآءَهُ لَمْ يَجِدْهُ شَيْئًا وَوَجَدَ ٱللَّهَ عِندَهُ فَوَفَّىٰهُ حِسَابَهُۥ وَٱللَّهُ سَرِيعُ ٱلْحِسَابِ}$$

And of those who disbelieve, their actions are akin to a mirage in the desert, that the thirsty assumes is water until when he comes to it, not does he find a thing, but finds Allāh with him, and He will pay him his full due; And Allāh is swift in settling the account.[69]

---

69 Sūrah An-Nūr 24:39

It is his perception that determines his state. For the believer sees the Unity of God. The disbeliever sees a multiplicity, and hence sees chaos and disorder, both within himself and external. He cannot distinguish between reality and fantasy. Regardless of either, 'existence' is that which the being can perceive and affirm. There is no such thing as 'perceiving' in a state of 'non-existence' because perception is the beginning whose end is a conscious affirmation or negation, and consciousness must exist to perceive.

This is why we say that man cannot comprehend 'non-existence' because he, as the 'being' must exist for his 'consciousness' to exist. Consciousness cannot exist if the being does not exist. And since the being did not exist, neither did his consciousness, with which he could neither affirm nor negate his state of non-existence. This contingency is vital, as the being must be consciousness to affirm its existence. The وُجُود is therefore a 'finding' best described as the 'intuition of existence.'

Let me explain this further. The ultimate knowledge is Knowledge of God. This Knowledge is a universal unity. A singular, wholesome knowing, without any partitions or compositions. It is the kind of knowing that is a direct reflection of God Himself as the ultimate unity. It is the knowing of *Tawhīd*. All other knowledge stems from this singular source knowledge in varied branches and partitions, such that as that knowledge expands, like the roots of a tree permeating into the ground, each root is seemingly different from every other. Humankind is thus imprinted with that singular knowing in his very nature, *Fitrah*. This knowing can only be realized in the Divine Presence, for that is a presence of wholesome unity. There are no particulars and semantics, facts and figures, possibilities and probabilities in that Presence. Only the Absolute Truth, which is a universal truth not only across the material, observable world (the Universe), but across all the dominions of His creation. The pursuit of Knowledge, therefore, may seem to be a matter of accumulating as many particular and semantic facts and figures, but the real knowledge-seeker is on a path of realizing that universal truth, which in essence is a 'remembering' of what the being testified to in a state of pure *Fitrah*.

In other words, this is what he is looking for in existence, and this is what he will 'find' the more intuitive he becomes of existence. The more he understands the 'water' in which he is swimming for the entirety of his existent state.

Existence into two. God's Absolute Existence وجود المطلق, which is an existence distinct from the existence of all else. The existence of all else is dependent on the Absolute Existence of God, but it is not dependent on all else, which means all else exists *because* God exists. From the existence of all else, there are three categories. There is that which Exists in Form وجود الظاهري, as a real entity. Then there is that which Exists in Image وجود الذهني, as a concept in the mind. And that which Exists in Speech وجود اللغوي, as a symbol in language. We are only concerned with these three, as the Absolute Existence of God is beyond our scope of comprehension. We say that the latter two do not determine the first. Rather the first determines the latter two. Regardless, the latter two are still existent entities. One may envision, for instance, a Unicorn. One may even use the word 'Unicorn.' Both are existent in their respects, but not existent in form, or as an actuality. The only true existent entity is that which can exist in all three aspects, as a real entity, as a concept in the mind, and as a symbol in language. The mind has been enabled to consciously affirm or negate these three, and to distinguish them from themselves as well as from the Absolute Existence of God.

This is where you must focus your attention. To cultivate this inherent ability in contemplation of your own existence. And to aid you in understanding this 'water' you exist in, your mind also has the ability to contrast it to 'non-existence.' In that regard, you will be able to determine the significance of your existence, whether you are a 'thing' or not a thing. Whether you are 'something' or 'someone.'

'Non-existence' we have said, does not mean 'nothing'. Rather we argue that 'nothingness' is an existent entity. A 'thing' is said to be 'nothing' when it has no substance, form, essence, or purpose. It is said to be something when it has substance, form, essence, and purpose. Your 'being' is therefore a continual process of 'becoming' فيكون. You are an entity that is in a perpetual motion of change. The existence of an entity begins when He Almighty issues the command of كن, as 'BE.' Prior to which it exists as 'nothing' for it has no substance, form, or purpose.

Hence your Lord has said;

79

خَلَقَهُ مِن تُرَابٍ ثُمَّ قَالَ لَهُ كُن فَيَكُونُ

He created him [man] from matter, thereafter He said to
him, "Be!" and it became. [70]

You were then proportioned and given form;

فَإِذَا سَوَّيْتُهُ وَنَفَخْتُ فِيهِ مِن رُّوحِى فَقَعُوا لَهُ سَـٰجِدِينَ

So when I have proportioned him and breathed into him
of My Spirit...[71]

He then gave you purpose;

وَمَا خَلَقْتُ ٱلْجِنَّ وَٱلْإِنسَ إِلَّا لِيَعْبُدُونِ

And I did not create Jinn and Man but to serve Me.[72]

And thus you became 'Something' with form, substance, and
purpose. This was the process of your coming into existence from non-
existence, from being nothing to being something. You existed in the
purest form, the purest state. This is your 'pre-worldly' stage. It is in this
stage when that 'prime knowing' of the ultimate unity was imprinted
into your 'being' as a wholesome testimony;

وَإِذْ أَخَذَ رَبُّكَ مِنۢ بَنِىٓ ءَادَمَ مِن ظُهُورِهِمْ ذُرِّيَّتَهُمْ وَأَشْهَدَهُمْ عَلَىٰٓ أَنفُسِهِمْ
أَلَسْتُ بِرَبِّكُمْ قَالُوا بَلَىٰ شَهِدْنَآ أَن تَقُولُوا يَوْمَ ٱلْقِيَـٰمَةِ إِنَّا كُنَّا عَنْ هَـٰذَا
غَـٰفِلِينَ

And [remember] when your Lord took from the children
of Ādam, from their loins, their descendants, and made them
testify of themselves, [saying to them], "Am I not your Lord?"
They said, "Indeed, we testify." Lest you should say on the Day
of Resurrection, "Indeed, of this we were heedless." [73]

---

70 Sūrah Āl 'Imrān 3:59

71 Sūrah Sād 38:72

72 Sūrah Adh-Dhāriyah 51:56

73 Sūrah Al-A'rāf 7:172

This is the state of pure testimony and witnessing of the Divine Presence. It was a state in which the material, biological body you currently occupy had not yet been fashioned for you. You were not born yet. You existed in your ethereal body, your spiritual or essential body. In this state, every human being ever created was gathered in the Divine Presence and made to witness God Almighty. Here, He asked a question whose response could only be an affirmation. There was no room for reason. No negotiation or deliberation. Even so the question was asked أَلَسْتُ بِرَبِّكُم *"Am I not your Lord?"* to which one may affirm or negate if they so wished, but not a single individual negated. It was a pure testimony of affirmation, بَلَى شَهِدْنَا *"Indeed, we testify!"* because that state was a *Fitrah* state, and in the Divine Presence only the Absolute Truth prevails. Subjective positions, views, opinions, possibilities, or any such entity has no place. A state of pure *Fitrah* witnesses God Alone as the only Real and Absolute. As the only Truth.

But lest you then say, upon the finality of your becoming, that you were unaware of this testimony. Because there will arrive that moment, when you will once again be recalled into the Divine Presence, a presence in which only the Absolute Truth prevails, a presence in which you will not be able to deny whatever you denied in your life while in a state of delusion.

From this incredible juncture, the process continues as the 'being' takes on the Almighty's intended substance, form, essence, and purpose from being 'something' to becoming 'someone' worthy of account.

Understand then what is meant by Form, Substance, Essence, and Purpose. Your form is the human form. The shape, dimensions, extensions, and such. You have limbs, a head, a torso. They are functional entities with a material reality and an inherent purpose to your being. Your substance is what determines that form. The 'materials' whether earthly or ethereal that come together in their purest elements to build that form.[74] Your essence is that which vessels your being and occupies the form. It powers the form, gives it its function and parameters, and governs those functions and parameters.

---

74 We are not talking about 'atoms' 'molecules' 'quantum particles' and such. We are referring to that which makes the atoms and molecules. The elements that originate the matter.

Your purpose is the reason why He created you. This is what you want to truly realize. Everything else about you can be studied under scientia. The form can be observed and quantified. Its functions can be learned. Its essence can be theorized. But you, the *being*, why you were created, for what purpose did He originate you... *that* is what you are meant to realize. And this is not a knowledge gained from any book, writ, commentary, or theory. Even the one you hold in your hands cannot give you the answers. They are all but instruments to help facilitate the journey of knowing.

As a 'something' you are given a designation and destination in Time, you are allocated a measured duration in a preordained realm which determines your state of existence in that realm. Each individual enters this realm at a destined time and departs at a destined time. You thus enter this material realm which we call *Al-Ardh* الأرض, the material, observable universe, to serve a purpose. That purpose is to complete your 'becoming' فيكون as He intended. This is now your 'worldly' stage.

وَلَكُمْ فِى ٱلْأَرْضِ مُسْتَقَرٌّ وَمَتَٰعٌ إِلَىٰ حِينٍ

...and for you on the earth is a place of settlement and enjoyment [i.e., provision] for a time.[75]

قَالَ فِيهَا تَحْيَوْنَ وَفِيهَا تَمُوتُونَ وَمِنْهَا تُخْرَجُونَ

He said, "Therein you will live, and therein you will die, and therefrom you will depart."[76]

Now we will speak briefly on 'Purpose.'

Understand then that 'Purpose' is parted into two. The 'Purpose of Being' and the 'Purpose of Life.' The former designates the 'reason you were created', and the latter designates the 'reason you were sent into this world.' The latter purpose contributes to the fulfillment of the former purpose. The latter purpose is defined and limited to this earthly state of your being. Its fulfillment cannot be delayed or postponed. It must be realized with immediacy, prioritized above all else, and diligently

---

75 Sūrah Al-A'rāf 7:24

76 Sūrah Al-A'rāf 7:25

observed, for the continuum of your existence in the earthly realm is irreversible. Each passing moment is a moment lost in fulfillment of that purpose, and for lack of fulfilling the *purpose of life* results in a failure to fulfill the *purpose of being*.

Pay close attention then. For if you were to ask me, *"What is the meaning of life?"* I would respond with, *"Death."*

The meaning of life is unveiled at the moment of death. Death alone serves the purpose of life, in other words, you are alive for the sole purpose of dying. As death alone can transition your present state of existence into the next phase. Hence His saying, *'Therein you will live, and therein you will die, and therefrom you will depart.'*

And by its nature, this purpose of life cannot be fulfilled without guidance. The nature of the world is not simply a deduction of what the world and its constituents are. It extends further into understanding how to navigate it. For there are elements that contribute to the fulfillment of the purpose, and others that are detrimental to it. And since we have already established the truth that the world and its constituents cannot explain themselves, they cannot be relied upon to offer the guidance. The guidance must come from He who created the realm, for only He truly knows what it entails.

Thus His saying to Ādam and Hawā, and by extension to their descendants, the human race;

$$\text{فَإِمَّا يَأْتِيَنَّكُم مِّنِّي هُدًى فَمَنِ اتَّبَعَ هُدَايَ فَلَا يَضِلُّ وَلَا يَشْقَى}$$

...and if there should come to you guidance from Me, then whoever follows My guidance will neither go astray nor suffer.[77]

But this guidance is not unconditional. It is not simply a matter of following procedure. This *Sharīʿah* that He sends down as the guidance must be understood, the understanding of which is only arrived at upon realizing that universal absolute truth affirmed in that pre-worldly state. In other words, *Sharīʿah*, which is the Letter of the Law, cannot be established without *Tawḥīd*, which is the Spirit of the Law, the essential reason and purpose of adhering to that Law. This *Tawḥīd*

---

77 Sūrah Ṭāhā 20:123

is less a matter of drawing rational or logical conclusions and more a matter of remembering that universal testimony, such that the essence of the *Sharī'ah* is entwined with both 'knowing it' in its constituents and knowing *why* it should be followed. Without a complete realization of both, one deliberately misguides themselves, being blind to the very Light that would reveal their existence and its purpose.

Thus does He say;

وَمَنْ أَعْرَضَ عَن ذِكْرِى فَإِنَّ لَهُ مَعِيشَةً ضَنكًا وَنَحْشُرُهُ يَوْمَ ٱلْقِيَـٰمَةِ أَعْمَىٰ

And whoever turns away from My remembrance, indeed, he will have a depressed life, and We will gather him on the Day of Resurrection blind."[78]

قَالَ رَبِّ لِمَ حَشَرْتَنِىٓ أَعْمَىٰ وَقَدْ كُنتُ بَصِيرًا

He will say, "My Lord, why have you raised me blind while I was seeing?"[79]

قَالَ كَذَٰلِكَ أَتَتْكَ ءَايَـٰتُنَا فَنَسِيتَهَا ۖ وَكَذَٰلِكَ ٱلْيَوْمَ تُنسَىٰ

He [Allāh] will say, "Thus did Our signs come to you, and you forgot [disregarded] them; and thus will you this Day [as something] forgotten."[80]

In other words, insofar as your conscious life is concerned, where you, your thoughts, and the execution of your will are all preoccupied with the comings and goings of this world, whether they pertain its natural processes or societal norms and practices, you will not be concerning yourself with what you should be concerned.

The above remarks, if understood in their true aspects, should have a profound impact deep on your heart. God Almighty is provoking your thoughts with a sincere question; *Why should I give you any regard, when in your life I was just an option?*

---

78 Sūrah Ṭāhā 20:124

79 Sūrah Ṭāhā 20:125

80 Sūrah Ṭāhā 20:126

Where are your priorities?

As when the moment of death arrives, when you are in that state of true realization, when the meaning of life is now being unveiled to you... what will you do? What *can* you do?

For death is certain. It is, in perspective, the most certain thing in your life. Everything else can be relatively regarded. Circumstances shift, things happen in different scales and magnitudes, various effects ensue from various causes as and when the variables and conditions change, such that outcomes can be necessarily determined, or elevated in a field of possibilities, or even regarded as impossible, but *Death*... is an absolute necessity. It *will* occur. It bears no possibility or impossibility, and while in life every action you perform, every thought you formulate may be influenced by different sources, guided by different hands, even assisted in their executions, death is the only real action you will perform and experience entirely by yourself. No one can teach you how to die. No one can tell you what it entails. No philosopher, no book, not even this one, can give you a disposition as to what that moment and its realization truly entails.

Thus does He Almighty say;

$$وَجَآءَتْ سَكْرَةُ ٱلْمَوْتِ بِٱلْحَقِّ ۖ ذَٰلِكَ مَا كُنتَ مِنْهُ تَحِيدُ$$

And the intoxication of death will bring the truth; that is what you were trying to avoid.[81]

$$فَلَوْلَآ إِذَا بَلَغَتِ ٱلْحُلْقُومَ ۞ وَأَنتُمْ حِينَئِذٍ تَنظُرُونَ ۞ وَنَحْنُ أَقْرَبُ إِلَيْهِ مِنكُمْ وَلَٰكِن لَّا تُبْصِرُونَ ۞ فَلَوْلَآ إِن كُنتُمْ غَيْرَ مَدِينِينَ$$

Then why, when it [the soul at death] reaches the throat. And you are at that time looking on. And We [Our angels] are nearer to it than you, but you do not see. Then why do you not [evade death], if you are not to be recompensed?[82]

---

81 Sūrah Qāf 50:19

82 Sūrah Al-Wāqi'ah 56:83-86

Thus is the meaning of life unveiled upon death. Which is why those who wasted away their life, when they realize that moment, attempt a bargain as a result of their denial;

حَتَّىٰ إِذَا جَاءَ أَحَدَهُمُ ٱلْمَوْتُ قَالَ رَبِّ ٱرْجِعُونِ ۝ لَعَلِّي أَعْمَلُ صَٰلِحًا فِيمَا تَرَكْتُ ۚ كَلَّا ۚ إِنَّهَا كَلِمَةٌ هُوَ قَآئِلُهَا ۖ وَمِن وَرَآئِهِم بَرْزَخٌ إِلَىٰ يَوْمِ يُبْعَثُونَ

Until, when death comes to one of them, he says, "My Lord, send me back! That I might do righteousness in that which I left behind." Nay! It is only a word he is uttering [it has no effect in meaning]; and behind them is a barrier until the Day they are resurrected.[83]

This moment now marks the completion of your 'becoming.' When you transformed from nothing to something, this was your pre-worldly stage of becoming. You then entered into this world as 'something' and your journey thus transformed you from something to someone. Someone, either worthy of praise, or worthy of blame. The finality of this journey, which is the moment of death, determines which 'one' you became, and each being will taste that moment. This tasting is called *Dhawq* ذوق.

كُلُّ نَفْسٍ ذَآئِقَةُ ٱلْمَوْتِ ۗ وَإِنَّمَا تُوَفَّوْنَ أُجُورَكُمْ يَوْمَ ٱلْقِيَٰمَةِ ۖ فَمَن زُحْزِحَ عَنِ ٱلنَّارِ وَأُدْخِلَ ٱلْجَنَّةَ فَقَدْ فَازَ ۗ وَمَا ٱلْحَيَوٰةُ ٱلدُّنْيَآ إِلَّا مَتَٰعُ ٱلْغُرُورِ

Every soul will taste death, and you will only be given your [full] compensation on the Day of Resurrection. So he who is drawn away from the Fire and admitted to Paradise has attained [his desire]. And what is the life of this world except the enjoyment of delusion.[84]

This is not a tasting of the senses, that is, not a tasting of the tongue. It is a tasting of the soul, of the highest aspect of 'sensitivity.' It is a taste

---

83 Sūrah Al-Mu'minūn 23:99-100

84 Sūrah Āli 'Imrān 3:185

that unveils pure truth, one that does not require any rational evaluation.[85] It is a first hand experience of reality as it reaches the being without the filter of the senses, and is a sensing done by the soul in which the soul is no longer 'protected' by its fleshy organic layer. For this reason, the pain is unlike any pain experienced, and the distortion that takes place, as highlighted in Qāf 50:19 above, what is termed as سكرة الموت a kind of 'intoxicated'[86] state that is not induced by material substance.

---

85 The experience of the being are of two kinds. That which is experienced through the senses, and that which is experienced intuitively without the senses. The kind of 'tasting' done by sensoria is of *absolute uncertainty*, which is to say the information generally perceived by the senses as a 'feel' or a 'taste' requires computation and interpretation. One typically deliberates it as saying 'It feels like such and such.' In this regard, the taste of death is of an *absolute certainty*. It does not 'feel like' anything. There is no likeness to its 'feeling' even though one may experience death-like cycles in life, such as sleep or unconsciousness. But the taste of death is absolute and unique. In other words, at the moment of its occurrence the being *knows* it to be death and nothing else. This kind of knowing is instantaneous, as is its affirmation of truth. In that moment, the Intellect is no longer linked to its rational counterpart, the Brain. As such, the mind does not undergo any algorithmic or logical process of rationalizing what the being is experiencing. The 'knowing' is intuitive and immediate, and the experience is unfiltered, such that it knows with absolute certainty what that moment entails. The same is true of the pain it experiences. The term *Dhawq* ذوق used in the Ayah is an eloquent articulation of that experience. It is a 'taste' of absolute certainty.

86 The word سكرة means 'intoxication'. One of its variants, سَكِر means "to be drunk", and سُكّر means "sugar" which is an essential ingredient in fermenting alcohol. Sugar, by its property, also induces a kind of euphoric sensation, particularly experienced by those who are not habitual to its effects. Children experience this euphoric state most, as it releases opioids and dopamine that induce a mild intoxication. The term is associated with death, because it bears the same, if not pronounced, symptoms. A state of intoxication is essentially a "desynchronization" of the soul-body link. In many cases, over-dosage of substance can induce death where the parting of the soul from the body is irreversible. The moment of سكرة الموت is a process of complete desynchronization that is not induced by substance, even if death was triggered by a substance. In the case of substance intoxication, only the bodily senses are distorted, but the soul itself has not crossed dimensions until death is caused (by overdose). However, in the case of سكرة الموت the body and its senses are completely detached, and the soul's senses are highly activated because it is quite literally crossing a dimension. This is why, in the *Ayah*, the term, *Dhawq* ذوق, is used as كل نفس ذائقة الموت , *'Every Soul shall taste death.'*

It is an intoxication that has no pleasure, a pain that is not sensorial, and a realization that is not rational.

The moment of death marks the finality of the 'becoming' process. One is now said to have become 'someone' worthy of categorization among those who will be permitted Paradise and the Divine Presence, or among those who will be cast into Hell and thus removed from the Divine Presence. This 'sorting' will be held in the grandest of all ceremonies. The Judgment.

This is now the fourth stage of your existence. Your being is redefined in a soul and body recreated.

As for the body, it was, in the worldly state, created as a finite and fragile entity. It was subjected to the decay of time. It was vulnerable to wear and tear. And most importantly, every extension of the body was made subservient to your will, so that your hands did whatever you intended of them, and did not oppose you. Your feet went where you directed them, and did not oppose you. Your tongue uttered what you instructed it, and did not oppose you. Hold this thought.

As for the soul, it was, in the worldly state, given to you as a balanced and proportioned entity. It had the faculty of Concupiscence, which served the role of governing the body's needs and wants. The faculty of Irascibility, which served the role of governing the body's defenses. And the faculty of intellection, which served the role of governing the concupiscence and irascibility faculties.

Both the body and soul were granted to the being, and the being was placed in a heart along with its will and consciousness. In that worldly stage, the consciousness served the role of affirming or negating what it ultimately perceived of reality. While the Will was granted certain parameters within which to execute. It was only free when it executed rightfully within those parameters. It lost its freedom when it attempted to transgress the boundaries. As such, the soul was proportioned with both vice and virtue, and the being was given the ability to decide between them.

وَنَفْسٍ وَمَا سَوَّىٰهَا ۞ فَأَلْهَمَهَا فُجُورَهَا وَتَقْوَىٰهَا ۞ قَدْ أَفْلَحَ مَن زَكَّىٰهَا ۞ وَقَدْ خَابَ مَن دَسَّىٰهَا

And the soul and how He proportioned it. He inspired it with vice and virtue. The one who succeeds is the one who purifies it [by choosing good]. The one who fails is the one who prevents it [from choosing good][87]

Understand then, that in this worldly state of its existence, the will has been given parameters of execution. It is not inherently 'free' as is loosely propagated. Rather it has inherent restrictions. It has been given a moderate measure of control, which to most seems boundless because they do not recognize the boundaries. Within these boundaries, it has choice. It can decide to become imprisoned, and that imprisonment is the imprisonment of the devils and those who become demonic. In the eternal prison, the abyss that is hell, the Will can no longer choose. Alternatively, it can decide to become free, and that freedom is the freedom of the Angels and those who become Angelic. In that eternal paradise, the Garden of Abode, the Will is unbound to choose whatever it so wishes to choose.

However, there is this intermediary state between the worldly existence that ends with death, and the eternal existence that begins with the end of judgment. This intermediary is the state of *Qiyām* قيام, or *Ba'th* بعث, or also termed as *Yawm ud-Dīn* يوم الدين.

Thus does the Almighty ask;

وَمَآ أَدْرَىٰكَ مَا يَوْمُ ٱلدِّينِ ۞ ثُمَّ مَآ أَدْرَىٰكَ مَا يَوْمُ ٱلدِّينِ ۞ يَوْمَ لَا تَمْلِكُ نَفْسٌ لِّنَفْسٍ شَيْئًا ۖ وَٱلْأَمْرُ يَوْمَئِذٍ لِّلَّهِ

And what can make you realize what is the Day of Recompense? Further, what can make you realize what is the Day of Recompense? It is the Day when a soul will not possess for another soul [the will to do] a thing; and the Will, that Day, is [entirely] with Allāh.[88]

You have no Will on that day. No one can come to your aid, even if they so will. Nor can you aid anyone, including yourself, even if you so

---

87 Sūrah Ash-Shams 91:7-10

88 Sūrah Al-Infitār 82:17-19

will. Your limbs are no longer subservient to you. Nor is your tongue, eyes, ears or any part of you. In this worldly state, they have all been made subservient to your Will. But on that day, they are all subservient to His Will. And He will instruct them to testify against you, and they will obey Him against your Will.

Your 'freedom' therefore, in this worldly life, is to recognize the limits of your Will, and to recognize that its freedom of execution is found in its submission to the Will of God. For you, as a being, have been inherently created a slave, but a slave who has been given the choice to serve whom he choses. You can choose to submit your Will to the world, to its frills and delusions, to your 'self' and its whims and desires, and thus does your Will become enslaved to the world. Or you can choose to submit your Will to the Will of God, and in doing so, not only will you become what He intended you to become, but you will free yourself from everything else.

That is *Free Will* in Islām.

THE LAMP
AND ITS
LIGHT

The month of Ramadhān is the Crucible of Abstinence in Time. It is the Sacred-most month, the holiest of holies, the sanctuary that safeguards from all action unworthy of the Divine Presence. It is, as the Holy Prophet said;

إِذَا دَخَلَ رَمَضَانُ فُتِّحَتْ أَبْوَابُ الْجَنَّةِ، وَغُلِّقَتْ أَبْوَابُ جَهَنَّمَ، وَسُلْسِلَتِ الشَّيَاطِينُ

When Ramadhān approaches, opened are the Gates of Paradise, and closed are the gates of Hell, and chained are the demons.[89]

Likewise the Heart is the Crucible of Abstinence in Man. It is the sacred-most, the holiest of holies, a sanctuary from that which is unworthy, safeguarded from the demons.[90] And in the same metaphor, the month of Ramadhān has its innermost dimension, one single night

---

89 متفق عليه Muwatta Mālik 692, Sahīh al-Bukhāri 3277, Sahīh Muslim 1079

90 So long as it is kept in a pure state and maintained as a sanctuary by the being

most commonly regarded as the 'Night of Power.' Few, however, recognize this as the 'Light' of the month. It is the night in which the 'Light' shines, the 'Light' that powers the entire month, and it is the 'Light' of the month because this was the night in which the 'Light' itself was sent down.

This 'Light', this 'Nūr نور' is the Speech of God Almighty, a revelation unto man that would bring him out of the darkness of ignorance and into the Light of Knowing.

Thus His saying;

$$ قَدْ جَآءَكُم مِّنَ ٱللَّهِ نُورٌ وَكِتَـٰبٌ مُّبِينٌ $$

Indeed there has come to you from Allāh a Light and a clear Book

$$ يَهْدِى بِهِ ٱللَّهُ مَنِ ٱتَّبَعَ رِضْوَٰنَهُۥ سُبُلَ ٱلسَّلَـٰمِ وَيُخْرِجُهُم مِّنَ ٱلظُّلُمَـٰتِ إِلَى ٱلنُّورِ بِإِذْنِهِۦ وَيَهْدِيهِمْ إِلَىٰ صِرَٰطٍ مُّسْتَقِيمٍ $$

Allāh guides by it those who seek His pleasure by the means of peace, and it brings them out of darkness into Light by His Permission, and it guides them to the Right Path.[91]

We say that 'darkness' does not exist as an entity. Just as well, cold, ignorance, and injustice, do not exist as tangible entities albeit their manifestations have some tangibility. And this is because they have no form, no substance, no essence, no meaning, no purpose. They are defined as the effects of the absence of those entities that have form, substance, essence, meaning, and purpose. Ignorance is the absence of Knowledge. Cold is the absence of Warmth. Injustice is the absence of Justice. And Darkness is the absence of Light.

In this regard, cold, injustice, and ignorance, are likened to 'darkness' because they are empty and void, meaningless and purposeless. They serve no benefit, and are themselves limited, finite, and temporal to a world of causation. This material, physical universe. They do not exist existentially, and when the Grand Trumpet is blown and all of creation undergoes its annihilation, they too will be annihilated as will whatever they manifest.

---

91 Sūrah Al-Mā'idah 5:15-16

On the other hand, warmth, justice, and knowledge, are likened to 'Light' because not only are they manifest and absolute, they are inherently meaningful and purposeful. They serve divine benefit, and are themselves unbounded, infinite, and eternal above and beyond the material, physical universe. They exist existentially, and when the finality of the realms occurs, they will endure.

And just as you would seek out this Night of Power, in which you are determined to seek closeness to the Divine Presence, so too should you seek out this Light within you, for it is this Light that will bring you closer to that presence. Because you, in this allegory, as a 'being,' are this point of light, originated from that pure light of creation. You, this point of light, have been shrouded with a conscious Will. This has been placed inside an 'Intellect' which has been shrouded with your thoughts and emotions, all of which have been assembled inside this crucible we call the Heart.

But this point of light is not 'self-illuminating'. It does not generate its own luminance. Which is to say the 'being' cannot explain itself, how it came to exist, *why* it exists. And it exists purely on the merit of knowing, for without the 'knowing', *id est,* without 'knowledge' the being cannot know how to exist, how to survive, or even why it should live. While the being can access the world through its sensorial layers and connect causes to effects to deduce something of reality by which it can live, the deepermost knowing of *'being',* the 'water' that we mentioned in the previous chapter, *that* it cannot unveil by its own intellection. *That* is a knowledge that must be inspired into him. This is what we mean when we say that the point of light is not self-illuminating. It must receive its sustenance of 'knowing' from a source other than itself, and that source is, by necessity, that which brought this point of light into being.

For if the being were self-illuminating, it could explain its luminance, in other words, you and I could issue a definitive statement of who we *really* are, where we came from and how we came to be, all without the need of an academic discourse. Without the need to *learn* it. It would be a knowledge already inherent in us, intuitive and recallable on the tongue, and would be the same knowledge in each and every being, without a difference of opinion, without suppositions or assumptions. It would be a knowledge that itself is acknowledged as an absolute knowing of both the being's existent and non-existent states. More so, if it were self-illuminating, it would have the ability to bring itself into existence, and just as well take itself out of existence at will, of which it can do neither.

We say that the One who originated the being from non-existence to existence is the sole providence for sustaining the luminance of the being.

Thus the Almighty's saying;

$$ اَللَّهُ نُورُ ٱلسَّمَٰوَٰتِ وَٱلْأَرْضِ $$

Allāh is the Light of the Heavens and the Ardh[92]. *He* is the illuminator of all the beings He has created. He sustains their luminance, their 'knowing' by which they are enabled existence. He alone can explain what He has created. In other words, whether directly or indirectly, *all* knowing is attributed to Him. As Light, by its inherent property, is that which reveals, and knowledge is likewise that which makes known the unknown by revealing it. Which is why we say of those who are knowledgeable that they are 'enlightened.' And if they are 'enlightened' then God Alone is the One who 'enlightens' them.

How then would you understand this Light? For surely, it cannot be likened to the 'light' of the sun. Or the moon. Or the flame of a candle. For that light cannot enter your inner most dimensions and ignite you from within. Rather none of these sources can even be called 'light' and we would say of them having only taken on the defining term as mere demonstrators of 'light'. For their luminance is foremost not their own. It is only an effect of a causal energy. But they do 'reveal' what is in darkness. These 'objects' in creation cannot be said to be 'Light' in the purest sense of the word. They are only mimicking the property of Light, which we have defined as that which reveals.

We say, that which sees itself and others is more worthy of the name

---

92   I have not translated the word الأرض here as "earth" as you would find in most translations, because the perception rendered is always the "planet" earth. And this is not what is denoted here. In my humble opinion, whenever the word الأرض is used by the Qurān in the phrase ٱلسَّمَٰوَٰتِ وَٱلْأَرْضِ, it means "the Heavens and the material realm" where الأرض in contemporary terminology would be "the physical and observable Universe". And Almighty Allāh truly knows best.

"Light." For if it only facilitates a seeing for others, but does not itself see, nor does it see itself, and likewise does not facilitate for others the ability to see themselves and further become illuminating for others, such an entity cannot be 'Light' itself nor its source, rather is a mere medium or carrier. And if at all it facilitates illumination, it does under instruction from Almighty Allāh, and He remains the Prime Illuminator.

This is because the word 'light,' in whatever human tongue, is but a linguistic expression for that through which unseen things are seen, as it would be for the objects in a dark room to remain concealed by its darkness until one lights a lamp through the effect of which the objects can then be seen. In a more profound sense, 'light' is that through which and for which things are unveiled and revealed.

In what way does it reveal? Rather, in what way does it illuminate the being, such that one can *see* what is being revealed? And further we ask, what is the greatest revelation of all, if not God? For He is the only True and Absolute, worthy of knowing. His revelation of Himself is the greatest revelation of all, in that everything else He reveals of His creation is but a Sign of His majesty. For the being to truly see the truth, he must long to see his Lord. But can he truly see his Lord with these organic spheres set into his skull? Nay! It is to see with the Heart. For the being is in the Heart, and the Heart was designed by the Creator to know Him! And so he sees his Lord by *knowing* his Lord, which is manifested by the Light which facilitates the knowing.

Thus does He Almighty elaborate what this Light truly is, in an allegory comprehensible to man;

$$\text{مَثَلُ نُورِهِ كَمِشْكَوٰةٍ فِيهَا مِصْبَاحٌ}$$

A profound metaphor of this Light, is like a niche مشكاة within which is a Lamp مصباح. It is a crevice in the wall, an architected pedestal set into the chest of man صدر, within which has been placed the lamp of intelligence عقل. This lamp, when it is lit, illuminates itself, the niche, and everything else within the reach of its glow. When it is not lit, it does not benefit anyone. And this lamp cannot burn without oil. It is the oil that soaks the wick. The purer its oil and the cleaner its wick, the stronger its flame and the brighter its luminance.

95

Liken this lamp to your intellect. Liken the glow of the lamp to your intelligence. Liken the flame to your being and its strength to your intellective power. Liken the oil to knowledge that feeds the flame of intelligence. If you *use* it, you illuminate your environs and those around you. If you do not use it, it will not benefit you nor others. For here you are, sitting in the darkness of ignorance, further deluding yourself of your ignorance when all you have to do is to light the lamp.

$$ ٱلْمِصْبَاحُ فِي زُجَاجَةٍ $$

The lamp has been placed inside a glass. This is its unique property. The glass is its protecting vessel. It safeguards the flame of the lamp from the extinguishing wind, from the fluttering moths. It protects the flame from impurities. Liken the glass to your Heart. And by this you will understand the reality of your being, as a point of light inside a lamp of the intellect in a glass orb as its vessel.[93]

$$ ٱلزُّجَاجَةُ كَأَنَّهَا كَوْكَبٌ دُرِّيٌّ $$

The glass is like a brilliant orb, a celestial body, a glowing star. It glows because of the lamp inside it. Its glow extends the luminance of the lamp. If the glass is kept cleaned, polished, removed of blemishes, it will allow more light to pass through it. If, however, the glass is unkempt, stained, blemished, it will diminish the lamp's glow. No matter how intelligent you may be, if your heart is not pure, it benefits no one. And glass by its inherent property, is opaque and dirty in its raw form. It must be molded and polished until it has lost its opaqueness, until it is so transparent as to allow light to pass through it without difficulty, and must be kept that way for it to continue glowing.

But as we said, this point of light is not self illuminating. Nor is the lamp, nor the glass. Your intelligence is not inborn. Knowledge is not

---

93 This radically challenges any human conception of the true nature of the human being, where contemporary sciences attempt to prove the existence or nonexistence, or at the very least provide even a rational explanation of consciousness, the mind, and the soul, from a materialistic approach using reductionist methodologies.

something that just pours out of you without you making the effort to use your intellect to acquire it, just as the wick must struggle to soak the oil and keep the flame alive.

يُوقَدُ مِن شَجَرَةٍ مُّبَـٰرَكَةٍ زَيْتُونَةٍ لَّا شَرْقِيَّةٍ وَلَا غَرْبِيَّةٍ

It is lit, this glass orb as is the lamp within it, by a Blessed Olive Tree. A pure tree. With the deepest roots. An absolute foundation. An unshakable trunk. Strong extending branches. Rich green leaves. Ripe olives sprouting from every bud. Where is this tree?

It is not of the east nor of the west. It is not of the realm of cardinal coordination. It exists *outside* this physical, material world.

يَكَادُ زَيْتُهَا يُضِىٓءُ وَلَوْ لَمْ تَمْسَسْهُ نَارٌ

The oil of its olive glows without being touched by fire. This oil is self-illuminating. This is knowledge in its purest form. So pure, it sustains itself. It validates itself. It authenticates itself. It does not need your science to prove its validity. It stands absolute in truth. This is the oil that the wick of your intellect needs to truly burn and glow with intensity so fierce as to diminish the darkness of ignorance. It burns without smoke. Without soot. Without impurity.

نُّورٌ عَلَىٰ نُورٍ

It is the Light of Revelation standing in eternal judgment over the Light of Reason. For while you may ignite your lamp with the knowledge of reason, *subjective* knowledge, *semantic* knowledge, *particular* knowledge, riddled with your theses and theories, your facts and figures, your numbers and equations, *that* light will always burn feeble and jittery, smoky and hazy. For us to say you are enlightened, your lamp must be ignited with the Knowledge of Revelation, *absolute* knowledge, *universal* knowledge, a knowledge that settles deep in the heart with a certainty that is unshakeable. This is the Light that is worthy of the word 'Light' for it reveals what no faculty of man, however refined, can ever reveal. It is a knowledge experience that is 'tasted' not by the senses, but by the Heart.

97

But this is not a knowledge acquired arbitrarily. It is not academia. It must be *earned* spiritually!

يَهْدِى ٱللَّهُ لِنُورِهِ مَن يَشَآءُ ۚ وَيَضْرِبُ ٱللَّهُ ٱلْأَمْثَٰلَ لِلنَّاسِ ۗ وَٱللَّهُ بِكُلِّ شَىْءٍ عَلِيمٌ

For Allāh guides His Light unto whomsoever He wills. One who proves himself worthy of that Light. One whose heart is honest and sincere. And thus does Allāh present such allegories for the sake of man's understanding. And He Allāh is of all things All-Knowing.

Those who seek His light are on a path of great difficulty. A path of struggle. A path that hones and molds, refines and disciplines the being in such a way as to purify the being. Because that Light is of purity. We say that there must be an intimate connection between the knower and the thing to be known. And it cannot be that one is pure and the other is not. For the being to know that Light of purity, he must himself become pure. Only when the heart is cleansed of its blemishes can that Light enter it and ignite the lamp, to reveal more than what the organic eyes can perceive, to see beyond the turbulences of this world, to see the peace and tranquility it longs for.

The Heart's contentment, and the being's fulfillment, is in that Light, an no place else. And the only place you will find that Light is in His Beloved Messenger (ﷺ), for this is a Light of the Prophetic Spirit, and he (ﷺ) is سراجا منيرا, a light-giving lamp.

THE
EPISTEMOLOGY
OF TRUTH

If we affirm that the Holy Prophet (ﷺ) is سراجا منيرا, a light-giving lamp, then we must also affirm that the mannerism of acquiring that light, ergo, the 'Epistemology' by which we may come to know the truth and to affirm that what we know is the truth such that our belief in that truth can be justified, *that* epistemology can only come from him.

Because consciousness is not computational nor a physical process that can be described by computation, what it does, and how it does it, cannot be measured as a product of neural connections, nor an effect of quantum causes.[94] Contemporary views, which have hence become the standards of propagating subjective truths, project computed technology onto human behavior, where they fabricate an "artificial intelligence" of programmed impulses and computations to suggest that as an allegory

---

94   Secularism uses a concept called "Orchastrated Objective Reduction" or "OrchOR", a biological philosophy of mind, to suggest that consciousness originates at the quantum level inside neurons. This is a flawed and delusional epistemology that employs "Reductionism" at its foundation, i.e to "reduce" that which is inherently existential to a physical and biological scale, and thus examined on that plane. This epistemology is no different than translating text from a source language and then interpreting the translation. It will always yield wrong results.

of how the human mind works. This flawed epistemology supposedly helps them "understand" how we, as an intelligent species, come to know what we know and how we know it. The likened similitude of this utterly foolish endeavor is to use the inside of a hat to understand why the head is spherical. I call it a foolish endeavor because the hat is effectually designed to fit the roundness of the head. The head is not spherically designed to fit the hollow of the hat.

Their assumption, and it always begins with this assumption, is that human nature is spontaneously adaptive, not inherently designed. That the mind at birth is *tabula rasa*, as likened to technology, like a blank drive to be filled with data, and that data is thus programmed formatively via a series of algorithms that adapt into whatever present paradigm is at play. We argue that human nature is 'preprogrammed' prior to birth with something termed as 'A-Priori Knowledge,' that the mind is already in possession of innate knowledge which defines the creature's role in the world. Not all knowledge is gained from sensorial experience, rather the sensorial experience is but a key to unlocking the knowledge already imprinted into man (knowledge of God), and not the source of knowledge itself. Further, we would assert, that essentially, no knowledge is derived exclusively from worldly experience, but that the experience only facilitates in knowing that which is deeply embedded into the Heart, the prime of which is the testimony availed when He Almighty asked أَلَسْتُ بِرَبِّكُمْ, *"Am I not your Lord?"*

Since at that stage, the being existed as an essence without its body, and the affirmative response was generated by the being, both question and its response were imprinted into the very nature of the being as an innate knowledge. This irrefutably proves that the *'Fitrah'* has a predefined intelligence that foremost affirms its Creator, after which it affirms its own existence, which is to say the being is consciously aware that it is alive and it wants to stay alive. It then affirms the state in which it is alive. It further affirms that its purpose is to be in a perpetual motion of knowing which will enable it to stay alive. Cumulative, this builds towards a certain epistemology that it must adapt while in the worldly state of existence, because in its knowing, it affirms that there is truth to be sought in a world that it has recognized to be equally populated with falsity.

Epistemology as a science is the study of 'episteme,' a system of understanding or a mannerism of knowing. It can be argued that there are various manners of knowing, but only one that successively avails the truth. In that regard, there are numerous epistemologies, and each one is used to define this journey of seeking the truth by entraining the intellect along a path, so that the seeking of truth ultimately becomes intuitive. The mind can be described as having an open field of vision as it recognizes multiple inroads of knowledge. Since it is integrated with the body, it can hold a conviction in sensory inroads as something tangible. However, the nature of the sensory world, as we said, is populated with truth as well as falsehood. The mind must therefore be able to distinguish between the two, which it cannot do intuitively unless it primarily defines the world it exists in and determines a safe and navigable path. If we liken the intellect to a ship in a sea of things to be known, some beneficial, others worthless, and yet others harmful, an epistemology can be likened to a navigational chart that outlines the safest route to the precious treasures, gems, and pearls of knowing.

The intellect, therefore, can deduce the outward nature of the world through sensorial probing and rational naming and categorization, but it cannot explain the essential or ontological nature of the world in the same way that it cannot explain its own essential nature because it did not originate the world nor itself. And we argue that any 'thing' in existence that cannot originate itself, rather is itself originated, cannot explain itself. For to have the ability explain itself, it must first have the ability to originate its own existence and equally remove itself from existence if it so wills. The realm then, and everything in it, including the human being, is an 'enclosed entity,' and therefore its essential knowledge must come from other than itself. This means that the mind requires parameters and limits as a 'guidance' that will enable it to recognize the limits of the enclosed entity so as to affirm where its truth can be derived and hence navigate the correct pathway to that source of truth. In other words, it need a correct epistemology.

An epistemology can be rationalized, its processes understood, the parameters defined, but even so, without attempting to rationalize it, so long as the being adheres to it, the epistemology can still guide him. The adherence will entrain the mind to think within the defined parameters, and will equally entrain the rest of the being to govern itself accordingly.

We argue that if God created man, and God is the only One who can guide man, then the only correct epistemology is that which is defined by Him. And since God has ordained a *Dīn*, we would then say that the correct epistemology is to be found embedded in the structure of the *Dīn* as the way of life.

Let us then examine it closely;

[This event occurred in the last eighty days of the Holy Prophet's life, and the event is narrated by one of his closest companions, Umar Ibn Al-Khaṭṭāb. I have placed the Arabic text in segments followed by my own translation, and my commentary and explanation of each section is in the footnotes]

عَنْ عُمَرَ رَضِيَ اللهُ عَنْهُ أَيْضًا قَالَ بَيْنَمَا نَحْنُ جُلُوسٌ عِنْدَ رَسُولِ اللهِ صلى الله عليه و سلم ذَاتَ يَوْمٍ إِذْ طَلَعَ عَلَيْنَا رَجُلٌ شَدِيدُ بَيَاضِ الثِّيَابِ شَدِيدُ سَوَادِ الشَّعْرِ لَا يُرَى عَلَيْهِ أَثَرُ السَّفَرِ وَلَا يَعْرِفُهُ مِنَّا أَحَدٌ حَتَّى جَلَسَ إِلَى النَّبِيِّ صلى الله عليه و سلم فَأَسْنَدَ رُكْبَتَيْهِ إِلَى رُكْبَتَيْهِ، وَوَضَعَ كَفَّيْهِ عَلَى فَخِذَيْهِ

Umar, may Allāh be pleased with him, also said;[95] *We were seated with the Messenger of Allāh, peace and blessings be upon him, on that day (that this event occurred). There appeared among us a man with brilliantly white robes and black hair. No trace of a journey could be seen on him, nor was he recognizable as one of us.*[96] *(He approached) Until he sat with the Prophet, peace*

95 This Hadīth is taken from Imām An-Nawawī's collection of Forty الأربعون النووية. Since the first Hadīth in the collection was narrated by Umar, this one follows as قال أيضا "he also said." The Hadīth متفق عليه is recorded in Muwatta Mālik, Musnad Ahmad, Sahīh Bukhārī, Sahīh Muslim, Sunan Nasāī, Sunan Ibn Majāh, Sunan Abī Dawūd, and Jamī At-Tirmīdhī.

96 This description is to emphasize that this occurrence took place in a such a precedence as to draw our attention to what is occurring. This individual was not a resident of Madīnah, nor was he a traveler. Where he came from immediately becomes a matter of intrigue, and that intrigue is held for the duration of the conversation that follows. It further signifies that what unfolds was, and continues to remain, a matter of paramount importance.

and blessings be upon him. And he placed his knees to his (the Prophet's) knees, and placed his palms upon his (own) thighs.[97]

وَقَالَ يَا مُحَمَّدُ أَخْبِرْنِي عَنْ الْإِسْلَامِ

فَقَالَ رَسُولُ اللَّهِ صلى الله عليه و سلم الْإِسْلَامُ أَنْ تَشْهَدَ أَنْ لَا إِلَهَ إِلَّا اللَّهُ وَأَنَّ مُحَمَّدًا رَسُولُ اللَّهِ، وَتُقِيمَ الصَّلَاةَ، وَتُؤْتِيَ الزَّكَاةَ، وَتَصُومَ رَمَضَانَ، وَتَحُجَّ الْبَيْتَ إِنْ اسْتَطَعْت إِلَيْهِ سَبِيلًا

قَالَ صَدَقْت فَعَجِبْنَا لَهُ يَسْأَلُهُ وَيُصَدِّقُهُ

He (the man) said (to the Prophet), "O' Muhammad, inform me about Islām."
The Messenger of Allāh replied, "Islām is to bear testimony that there is no God but Allāh and Muhammad is the Messenger of Allāh, and to establish Salāt, to pay Zakāt, to Fast Ramadhān, and to pilgrimage the House (Ka'abah) if it is in your means."
The man said, "You are correct."
And we found this astounding. He asks and affirms the truth.[98]

---

97 This mode of sitting is universally established in Islām as the etiquette of sitting when seeking knowledge. Thus, from the very beginning, as a non-verbal declaration, this is defined as a situation in which prime knowledge is being conveyed. This knowledge will thus define the epistemology. The epistemology for the Muslim therefore includes the bodily etiquette as part of the learning process.

98 It is strange because the act of questioning is typically done with the intent of receiving an answer to quench the inquiry, not to correct the response. In this circumstance, the questioner is a stranger and the one being questioned is the Prophet of Allāh (ﷺ). Why then would the questioner affirm the correctness of the Prophet's reply? The epistemology availed here takes on three layers. Firstly, the act of asking and affirming correctness is typically done by teachers. Hence, a correct epistemology must involve a teacher who can affirm the correctness of an inquiry. Further, knowledge itself is primarily an oral transmission. Its acquisition from text is tertiary, whereby the text itself must be orally explained. Lastly, the acquisition of knowledge is inherently a mode of inquiry which takes the outward form of questioning. Knowledge is received by actively asking for it, seeking it, or probing for it, of which there are five instruments that the mind is equipped with and these are embedded in language as What, How, Why, When, and Where.

قَالَ فَأَخْبِرْنِي عَنِ الْإِيمَانِ

قَالَ أَنْ تُؤْمِنَ بِاللَّهِ وَمَلَائِكَتِهِ وَكُتُبِهِ وَرُسُلِهِ وَالْيَوْمِ الْآخِرِ، وَتُؤْمِنَ بِالْقَدَرِ

خَيْرِهِ وَشَرِّهِ

قَالَ صَدَقْتَ

He (the man) said, "Then inform me of Imān."

He (the Prophet) said, "That you believe in Allāh, and His angels, and His scriptures, and His messengers, and the HereAfter, and you believe in the Decree (His Divine Decree) its good and its bad" [99]

The man said, "You are correct."

---

99 Note that in both this and the first question, the Prophet (ﷺ) did not give a *definition* of Islām and Imān, which is contrasted to the other two questions that followed. This is because Islām does not *need* a definition. The word itself إسلام carries the meaning of 'submission,' and it is defined by Almighty Allāh Himself in the Qurān as إِنَّ الدِّينَ عِنْدَ اللَّهِ الْإِسْلَامُ (Āli 'Imrān 3:19) that the mode of existence for the human being is to Submit. The question then arises, "To what does one submit?" If we say that man is inherently created a slave, then he can never truly be a master, and he must submit to something. If we also say that man is inherently created to seek contentment, which he can only gain through freedom, then there must be something that can free him. This then becomes a relative matter. If he submits to other than God, he will be freed from God, but since everything is in a perpetual state of decay كُلُّ شَيْءٍ هَالِكٌ إِلَّا وَجْهَهُ (Qasas 28:88), the one who submits to other than God will find themselves submitting to that which does not last. Hence, if one submits *only* to God, he frees himself from everything else and lasts with the Everlasting. Islām is therefore understood as *'Submission only to Allāh'* and hence the one seeking to submit need only know *what* and *how* to submit.

Likewise, Imān does not need a definition, for belief is an innate attribute of the being. The Heart has been configured with only two qualities, to *know* and to *believe*. Imam Al-Laqqānī in his *Jawharat At-Tawhīd* versifies Imān as وفسر الإيمان بالتصديق, that Imān is understood as conviction constitutionally ratified by the Heart, and such a conviction cannot be given a linguistic definition as to what it is. Rather *what* to believe in must be defined. And the affirmation to both responses by the questioner establishes the boundaries of the components defined in each, in that they do not fall short, nor exceed the defined tenets, or *Pillars* as they are commonly known. If one is to be a Muslim and Mu'min, they must fulfill *all* the tenets of Islām, and likewise of Imān.

104

قَالَ فَأَخْبِرْنِي عَنْ الْإِحْسَانِ

قَالَ أَنْ تَعْبُدَ اللهَ كَأَنَّكَ تَرَاهُ، فَإِنْ لَمْ تَكُنْ تَرَاهُ فَإِنَّهُ يَرَاكَ

The man said, "Then inform me about Ihsān."

The Prophet replied, "That you serve Allāh as though you can see Him; and if you cannot see Him, know that indeed He can see you." [100]

---

100 Here we see a definition given, and this is because it *needs* a definition. The science that predominantly pertains Ihsān is called تصوف *Tasawwuf,* whose common translation as 'mysticism' and 'Sufism' is false and unjust. *Tasawwuf* is incredibly broad and incorporates numerous methodologies, some of which are erroneous, misleading, and delusional. The reason for there being numerous methodologies, as elaborated by Sidi Ahmad Zarrūq in his *Qawā'id At-Tasawwuf,* is that Ihsān begins with sincerity in the heart, and each one's sincerity differs from every other, hence each one attempts their own approach to draw closer to God Almighty. In this regard, not every approach is a true approach or will yield true results, hence for any approach to be given validity and acknowledged in its authenticity, its parameters must be adhered to as is defined by the Holy Prophet (ﷺ). The higher degree of 'seeing' Allāh is called مقام المشاهدة, defined as تعبد الله كأنك تراه "Serving Allāh as though you can see Him." This a 'seeing' of the Heart, not of the physical eyes, and is only achieved when one has mastered the lower degree called مقام المراقبة, defined as تعبد الله لأنه يراك "Serving Allāh knowing that He is seeing you." In essence, Ihsān is servitude to God alone with sincerity and honesty, by 'seeing' His Unity and Ordainment in all things, and if that is unattainable, the servant must be consciously aware that God is always watching him. As such, in whatever one does, they must ensure piety and righteousness, dedicating that service to Almighty Allāh. This cannot be achieved if one has not fulfilled the degrees of Islām and Imān, which is why it is not the first and second, rather it is the third but all-encompassing degree. *Tasawwuf* becomes the instrument that facilitates the accomplishing of this degree, but does not become the degree itself. For one may call themselves 'Sufi' but are not practicing Islām in its proper constituents, nor is their Imān true but that they have deluded themselves into believing that religion entails being in a mystified state. Likewise, one cannot call themselves '*Muhsin*' if they are doctrinally and dogmatically devout, but are impure within, such that their deeds and actions are selfish and egocentric. Being a true Muslim entails not just practicing religious rites, but having a firm belief in God Almighty and the tenets of creedal convictions, whether or not they can be rationalized, and further to that it entails piety, righteousness, being aware and cognizant of ones spiritual weakness, and actively striving to purify their spiritual states.

قَالَ فَأَخْبِرْنِي عَنِ السَّاعَةِ

قَالَ مَا الْمَسْئُولُ عَنْهَا بِأَعْلَمَ مِنْ السَّائِلِ

The man said, "Then inform me about the Hour."
The prophet said, "The one being questioned does not know any
more than the one questioning." [101]

قَالَ فَأَخْبِرْنِي عَنْ أَمَارَاتِهَا

قَالَ أَنْ تَلِدَ الْأَمَةُ رَبَّتَهَا وَأَنْ تَرَى الْحُفَاةَ الْعُرَاةَ الْعَالَةَ رِعَاءَ الشَّاءِ يَتَطَاوَلُونَ فِي الْبُنْيَانِ

The man said, "Then inform me of its indicatives."
The Prophet said, "The slavegirl will give birth to her mistress, and
you will see the barefooted, naked, destitute shepherds competing
in construction." [102]

---

101 While the apparent object of query is the 'Hour' referring to the Final Hour of temporal existence, within it is embedded the concept of Time. There being a 'final' hour dictates that there was an initial hour, and a passage between them. The 'Hour' is parted into two. The Greater Hour الساعة الكبرى, to the finality of all temporally existent entities and temporality itself, and the Lesser Hour الساعة الصغرى, to the finality of each individual entity in temporal time. What this means is that each entity is existent in Time, had an initiation in Time, and will have a finality in Time. Time is therefore the 'water' in which one exists, and in it is the being's journey and the destination. For mankind has only two prime questions as they pertain his existence. Who am I? What is my destiny? These two queries of Identity and Destiny seek to unravel his *Being* and his *Existence*. For him to realize his Being, he must understand Time, for he is existent *in* Time. Not in Space or Matter. We will discuss this in the next chapter.

102 Note that he (ﷺ) did not speak of 'major' signs that are paramount to the finality of human existence. He has, in other narrations, explicitly stated that the Hour would not be established until the Son of May descends, which implies that the Hour would not be established until Dajjāl makes his entry, and likewise until the Rightly-Guided Imam Al-Mahdi has established the *Khilāfah*. In this statement of his, he is identifying those elements that are pertinently detrimental to the being. When quantity is placed above quality, and when man is entrenched in material pursuit.

ثُمَّ انْطَلَقَ فَلَبِثْتُ مَلِيًّا

Thereafter the man left, and I remained for a while...

ثُمَّ قَالَ يَا عُمَرُ أَتَدْرِي مَنْ السَّائِلُ

قُلْتُ اللَّهُ وَرَسُولُهُ أَعْلَمُ

قَالَ فَإِنَّهُ جِبْرِيلُ أَتَاكُمْ يُعَلِّمُكُمْ دِينَكُمْ

Subsequently the Prophet said, "O' Umar, do you know who the questioner was?"
I said, "Allāh and His messenger know best."
He said, "Indeed, that was Jibrīl. He came to you, to teach you, your Dīn."

[Hadīth متفق عليه recorded in Muwatta Mālik, Musnad Ahmad, Sahīh Bukhārī, Sahīh Muslim, Sunan Nasāī, Sunan Ibn Majāh, Sunan Abī Dawūd, and Jamī At-Tirmīdhī.]

This is the Epistemology of Truth. It is the essential 'algorithm' which when entrained into the mind, whether or not one can rationalize the process, will *always* yield the truth. It carries the being from the outward manifestation of its reality, to the firm conviction it requires, deep into a spiritual state of intelligence, enabling it to arrive at that which will both enlighten it and strengthen it.

Fundamentally, the science of Epistemology seeks to understand the process of 'knowing.' How we come to know what we know, and how we establish that 'knowing' as the truth such that belief, of conviction in it can be justified as a 'true belief.' The diversity in human beliefs, both macro and micro,[103] presents itself as a collection of various truths, each one convicted in their understanding of what the truth is. If we only examine "faith" objectively, we find that the Christian is as faithful as the Muslim, and so is the Jew, Hindu, Buddhist, even the atheist and whatever else. Each one is convinced that their truth is *the* truth.

---

103 Macro in the sense of entire religions and world-views. Micro in the sense of sectarian divisions within those religions, or ideologies and philosophies parted from religion itself.

Secular epistemics, if at all they have an episteme, conclude in this regard by saying that the truth is subjective. Each one determines what is true to them, and the same applies even to sciences supposedly not affiliated with religion, in which different views and opinions, other than those that have been empirically and factually proven, are all subjective and equally true. Each one is entitled to their own version, and each version is to be 'respected' in their own respect, and only that which is empirical, such as the empiricism of secular sciences, remains the dominant judge of all these versions. That which is coherent with scientism is given civil regard, and that which is not is given cultural, ethnic, tribal, or primitive regard.

We counter this position by saying that *the Truth* is universal, not multiple and particular. *The Truth* is not a composition of facts and figures, which is to say that *the Truth* is not established on facts, rather facts are derived from *the Truth*. It is absolute, universal, and existential. It must be *'arrived at,'* not *'determined by,'* nor *'established'* by an arbitrary vote based on circumstantial paradigm shifts in human history. For facts are human derivatives. A fact is an arbitrary expression of what something is. It is a fact that the sky is a blue canopy over the earth, but also a fact that the sky is not an actual canopy with blue as its color. Both are expressions of the same entity, and both are factually true, because both have been derived from the truth of the entity. The truth exists independent of the facts derived from it. The truth can only be True. It cannot change to become false. But facts can change, and the same facts that are regarded as true can equally deceive, as the blueness of the sky can become gray, and what is perceived of it as a calcified ceiling can become a penetrable expanse.

If the truth can only be *'arrived at,'* there can only be one path of arrival. The journey itself may be longer or shorter, simple or difficult, for the resilience of different individuals are tested in different ways, but the *path* that we know as *Sirāt al-Mustaqīm* صراط المستقيم is only one. On this path, the journey of seeking knowledge is twofold. First, the soul must strive to arrive at *meaning*. Its arrival does not imply that it has gained knowledge, but that it has reached the threshold. Thereafter, it is granted an opening which allows meaning to arrive at the soul.

The success of this journey is determined by how well the journeyman is equipped, for which they must have all *four* requisite rations.

As there are those who only adhere to *Fiqh*[104] in fulfillment of Islām, but lack in others. These are bound to fall into hypocrisy.

There are those who only cling to *Aqīdah*[105] in fulfillment of Imān, but lack in Islām and Ihsān. These become doctrinally prejudicial.

There are those whose religion only entails *Tasawwuf*[106] in fulfillment of Ihsān. These are deluded.

There are those who only adhere to *Ma'ād*[107] in satisfying curiosity and phantasmal imagery. These are heedless wanderers.

I am not belittling the Jurists, nor the Theologians, Spiritualists, and Eschatologists. I am emphasizing that religion is not piecemeal, rather it is wholesome. And for one to have a proper epistemology to the truth, they must enclose themselves with all four. The proper epistemic pathway must be built foundationally and coherently. And the foundation is the

104 They foremost regard 'Fiqh' as mere jurisprudence, and that makes their entire projection of *Dīn* as being just legislative and political. They are lost in the particulars of *Fiqh*, of permissibilities and prohibitions, such that their outlook of existence becomes binary, and they find themselves unable to adapt to changing circumstances. In that regard, they have no firm grounding, and are themselves swayed by circumstantial shifts.

105 Their entire focus is doctrinal. Their projection of *Dīn* is an opinionated one. To them, the religion is truth based only on what they believe to be true. They are lost in creedal conflicts, such that their outlook of existence becomes egocentric, and they find themselves stubborn against the understandings of others.

106 Their entire focus is esoteric. Their projection of *Dīn* is mystical. To them, the religion is a fantasy of 'special powers' granted only to 'special people' with 'special spiritual ranks.' They are lost in phantasms of their own generation, such that they are in states of delusion of which they are unaware of. They give Spirituality the undeserving negativity that results in distorting the religion for those who are truly seeking spiritual guidance.

107 These are even more deluded than the rest, detached from the very foundations of religion. Their projection of reality is *"the world is ending, everyone is wrong, there is a great conspiracy afoot, we are enlightened to the truth, the rest are all sheep."* They are the most astray because they have no grounding in the fundamentals, have no creedal conviction, nor are they spiritually cleansed. Their litmus test is a very simple one. They will hardly be affected by the recitation of the Qurān, because they do not understand it in its language or its meanings. But they tend to become highly excited upon the notion of conspiracies of which they believe only they have the intellectual acumen to unravel.

Creed, followed by the Guidance, to enable a Spiritual cleansing, such that the Heart and Intellect are enlivened to penetrate the unfolding future towards the finality of human history.

One cannot grasp the eschatological unfolding without the Light to navigate its darkness, which is impossible to acquire without a spiritually cleansed heart, which itself cannot be done without the guidance that the Deliverer of the Light has sent down, and for this guidance to be implemented it must be understood, which cannot be done unless there is a firm conviction in that guidance to be true *before* any attempt to rationalize it is done.

The poetic principle is thus;

وقدم الأهم إن العلم جم	والعمر طيف زار أو ضيف ألم
أهمه عقائد ثم الفروع	تصوف وآلة بها شروع
حتى الباب الكبير	يفتح بمفتاح الصغير
فجهل الجاهل	وعرف العارف
إن العلم ينكشف بالخطاب	ونزله في لسان العرب
فالعربية مفتاح الأسرار والإعجاز	هذا معرج المعراج وميز الإمتياز

And such as it was availed, that the most crucial was knowledge. For life is but a passing guest and a spectrum of toil. The most important (step) is your creed, then come the branches of practice. Follow this with rectification of the 'self' and cleansing of the Heart. Then pick an instrument and begin the journey of knowing. Even the greatest door can be unlocked with the smallest key. For whoever is ignorant will remain ignorant. But the one who knows... Knows. That the Divine Speech unveils all knowledge, and it was sent down in the tongue of the Arabs. Thus Arabic is the key to its secrets and marvels. And this is the ladder of ascension, the distinction of excellence.[108]

---

108   The first two lines are from the Mauritanian scholar Murābit Ahmad Fāl al-Mutallī (d.2021) a student of Murābit Al-Hajj. The few great exemplars of our age, and may Allāh have mercy on them both.
The rest of the lines are my own additions.

The *Faqīh* must therefore have *Tasawwuf*, and the *Sūfi* must likewise have *Fiqh*. Without *Fiqh*, the *Sūfi* is deluded. Without *Tasawwuf*, the *Faqīh* is aimless. And both must have *Aqīdah*, without which they are both astray. Neither of these can be accomplished without proper study, the doorway to which is the Arabic language. For the knowledge is contained the Speech of God, which is قُرآنا عربيا.

This is why the *Dīn* is complete only with Islām, Imān, Ihsān, and As-Sā'ah. Where do these conform in the human being?

~ Islām deals with the 'being' in his outward manifestation by rectifying the aspect of the soul that is linked to the body. This is comprised of the Irascible and Concupiscent faculties which, when governed correctly, will maintain the body at optimal performance and efficiency. Their proper governance is contingent on the Will's inclination. The Will, as we said, has a choice. To submit to these worldly aspects or to submit to the Will of God. Submission to the worldly aspects enslaves the being. Submission to the Will of God is Islām, and Islām thus disciplines these two lower faculties of the soul in their link to the body. Which is why, as you notice, the Prophet (ﷺ) did not give the definition of Islām. He gave the components of submission, all of which pertain to the body. They are physical actions. And these physical actions performed at their ordained times in their ordained mannerisms override whatever inclinations the body and self may have at that time.

This is the entrainment of the Body and its sensoria to the Soul.

~ Imān deals with the 'being' in his interim manifestation. In the 'in-between' of the realms, which is the intellect and soul placed between sensoria (form and symbol) and the Heart (essence and meaning). It regulates the mind's intellection to keep it within safe parameters and boundaries, to ensure it does not tarry off on its own volition into estranged tangents that steer off the Right Path. This is of paramount importance which is why in the versification above, we say أهمه عقائد, the most important of all is *Aqīdah*. The mind *must* be regulated in its intellection so that *it* can then regulate the rest of the soul. Hence you notice, the Prophet (ﷺ) did not give the definition of Imān. It is understood as 'conviction.' *What* you hold a conviction in is what

111

matters, hence his delivering the components of Imān. For these are no physical entities. They are not tangible. They cannot be proven through the rationality of *scientia*. And the animalistic nature of the mind is to seek out 'empirical proof' of things, which in one aspect is an asset, but in existential matters is a liability. In this regard, it *must* be entrained to uphold belief before rationality. It *must* be entrained to recognize the Light of Revelation above the light of its own reason.

This is the entrainment of the Soul and its intellection to the Heart.

~ Ihsān deals with the 'being' in his inner manifestation. In the realm of essence and meaning, *Ālam Al-Amr* عالم الأمر. It regulates the heart and its focal point, since the heart, by its nature, is ever turning.[109] It is ever in a perpetual oscillation of trying to establish that direct connection with the Divine Presence it was once in, and is constantly turning and oscillating between this realm and the other. It is also exposed to, and affected by the causality of this world that blemishes it. This stains the heart, such that even in those moments when it is aligned to the Light, the Light is distorted, even prevented from entering it. These blemishes must be removed. Hence the dimension of Ihsān. Note here, the Prophet (ﷺ) provides us with a definition. It is to *see*, not with the eyes, but with the Heart, the Divine Presence. This is called *Maqām al-Mushāhadah* مقام المشاهدة, the rank of 'witnessing' which is the same 'witnessing' the heart experienced when asked to testify (Al-A'rāf 7:172). If you cannot *see* Him, know that He can see you, and this is called *Maqām al-Murāqabah* مقام المراقبة, the lesser rank of observance, meaning you are, whether you acknowledge it or not, always in a state of being observed. In other words, be the best that you can be, whether or not you can see the Almighty. Ihsān begins with *Ikhlās* إخلاص, sincerity in intention and action, such that righteousness is manifested, and it is to maintain consistency in righteousness even after the Heart is purified.

This is the entrainment of the Heart and its intentions to the Spirit.

---

109 This is derived from the semantic fields of the word قلب, one which means 'turning' or 'toppling'. Because the being has been placed in an interim and temporal state of existence, the heart is exposed on one side to the decaying material realm, and on the other to the everlasting spiritual realm, and is hence constantly turning between the two.

Then, and only then, can one truly come to the dimension of Time. For this now deals with the 'being' in his innermost. It unveils the channels of investigating its 'being'. Its existence. Its purpose. Its destination in Time. For it is a 'being' in 'Time'. It has an alloted period of time, a time of arrival, and a time of departure. Understanding 'Time' helps the being understand its 'being.'

You find here that 'eschatology' is but a minute component of Time, as it only pertains the finality of human history. There is yet the beginning of human history in addition to its vast continuum. This is the Epic of Man. The Epic of the Human *being*. Note then what the Prophet (ﷺ) has given you. Two indicatives of the finality of human history which are also indicatives of the 'being' far removed from his *being*. An age where quantity and materiality is what dictates quality and spirituality, which is the slave girl giving birth to her mistress. An upsetting of the natural order that is ordained by the Almighty, an order that was spiritually established, where the *Amr* gives rise to the *Khalq*, where the intentions are what dictate the actions and their manifestations. We are, in the present-future continuum, submerged in an age where few are able to identify this unnatural upheaval. Secularism now dictates that quantity must determine quality. The value of reality is not determined by reality itself intrinsically, rather it is determined by fabricated thing, notions, and ideals. It is an age in which materialism determines what should qualify as 'spiritual'. The created form determines its function. The action determines its intention. It is an age where everything is epistemologically flawed such that falsehood now appears as truth. Which gives rise to another phenomenon, where the beings are competing in material progress. Success is determined by increase, and increase is measured by quantity, the quantity of which is material. Rather than compete for spiritual growth, man is focused entirely on material pursuit, where they now ignorantly compete in constructing the tallest buildings to rival the heavens.

And you *are* engaging in these pursuits heedlessly. You think yourself alienated from the provinces of profane profits, but you are not. You think yourself intellectual when you achieve what the sacrilegious world endorses, when you see with your eyes how much quantity they have and you crave it so much so that their recognition of your achievements puts a smile on your face. You may be performing your worshipful acts, having understood the creed to its finest particular, even engaging in righteous deeds and actions, but all your pursuits in life fall short of you realizing who you truly are and what your created purpose is.

What *are* you really, other than a cog in the industrial machine geared towards engineering paradise on this terrestrial plane in manifest challenge to the Sovereignty of the Almighty? Can you truly claim to have the truth when you rejoice in their flawed epistemologies and are so far removed from His ordained epistemology?

If you are a *thing,* you are not a *being.*

Realize your *being.*

Don't become a *thing.*

TIME
AND
ETERNITY

We begin this chapter on the premise that 'everything that has a beginning, has an end,' for if there is a finality, there must be an initiation.

And thus, when this 'beginning' begins, there must be a marker to indicate its beginning. Something by which this beginning can be identified. And since it has a beginning, it will also have a progressive continuum. Along this continuum, every notable milestone also bears a marker. 'Tracking points' that guide as well as document each occurrence. And what we mean by this is that there must be 'something' that initiates the continuum, and allows its due process to unfold until it arrives at its zenith.

Following the limitless existence of the Divine Creator Himself, this particular principle is the first that comes into existence, and is the last to expire. It is the most confounding, the most perplexing, not only because it is both quantitative as well as qualitative, but that its quantity is a mere trace of its quality. Its quantity is only quantitative to the perceiver in his dimension, whereby its quality is boundless across all other dimensions. Its quantity is precise and calculable, whereby its quality is outside all rational comprehension.

Regarding the Creator, He Commands and Controls it to its absolute, but regarding the creation:

It is neither bound to, nor does it bind, yet everything that exists is shackled to it with absolute dependency. And even then, it does not regard itself to be 'in charge' by any virtue, for it is neither animate nor inanimate. It does not authorize, nor is it authoritative, yet without it there is no authority. It does not decide, nor can it be decided upon, and yet without it no decision can be made. It cannot be manipulated, nor is it manipulative, and yet without it nothing can be manipulated.

Recognize here that what we are talking about is a principle above and beyond anything we can know or even try to know. All I have done, in mention of the few points above, is to provoke your thinking with regards to Time in an attempt to take you out of its quantitative confines and plunge you into its qualitative realm.

Man is a sensorial creature, and this distinguishes him from the inanimate genus, as things that are inanimate do not have the ability to actively probe reality. In the animate genus, Man's sensoria awards him with perception which distinguishes him from the vegetative genus. His perception further awards him with intellection, which then distinguishes him from the animal genus. Regardless of all that, his sense and perception with reality is parable with his perception of earth and is inseparable from the earthly dimension so long as he is alive.[110] As he gazes out to the night sky and envisions other stars and planets, he calculates and concludes something of them in likeness to his own environs by "translating" his perception of reality to a 'human scale.' The unit of measure is always founded on what he can immediately perceive, and his assumption of all other reality beyond his physical reach is based purely on external vision, which in the end remains just that— an assumption. The correctness of his conclusion will depend entirely

110 In this, it is truly remarkable that many will experience a "strangeness" to their perception of time in interim stages of their lives, in sleep states or in states of illness, states in which their essential perception is stronger than sensorial perception, but will often dismiss or entirely forget those experiences when they return to their sensorial perception. Unbeknownst to them that their true realities are unveiled only when they are cut off from their outward senses, and that includes a true reality of space and time.

on the correctness of his assumption. His formulated equations, within their closed principles may be correct, but if his preceding assumptions are flawed, his resultant conclusions will also be flawed. For we may say that a quantity of one paired with another quantity of one is equivalent to a quantity of two is correct, the truth of the matter depends on whether we assume that 'one' is a unified quantity and pairing it with another is cumulative. But the same equation does not hold true for all circumstances. Two apples cannot become one, but two liquids can become one. In the former, one and one must be two, but in the latter, one and one become one. In both instances, the preceding assumptions must be true for the conclusions to be true.

The same is true of an outward perception of Time. Man's understanding of Time, regardless of how he formulates his equations, will depend entirely on his assumption.

That, in his rational deliberation of the observable universe, drawn from the underlying premise that it all began with the parting of a single point, he can calculate the temporal distance between then and now to a near approximation. But he is unrealizing of his crucial epistemological mistake. He calculated it based on his perception from earth. He assumes that since Space and Matter began at a certain point, that point being an occurring event, so too did Time begin at the same point. And if all three began at the same point, all three are relative to each other. The conclusion that all three are relative depends on his assumption that all three began at the same relative point.

As such, the quantity of 13.8 Billion 'years' is purely an arbitrary calculation. It may be factually correct, if at all, but it bears no real meaning or purpose. The number itself has no existential value, for all it truly conveys to the heart is 'a large quantity of time'. And it bears no significance to the heart, because the Heart not only has no interest in quantity, it was never designed to comprehend quantity. The number itself is a mere symbol which can be expressed as '13.8' or 'Thirteen-point-eight' or whatever other symbol employed to convey the same quantity, neither of which is of paramount importance other than to provide a rational reference that the mind can interpret and utilize in its orientation of reality. This figure itself only serves as a *count* of Time. It cannot be said to be *Time* itself.

We affirm that Time is not a unit. It is not an object. It is not a tool. It is not a dimension. It is not a yardstick. For if we say that Time is an object, and every object is made of matter that occupies space, then Time would not be called 'Time,' since it would be categorized as 'Matter' occupying space. What we have, what we use, as years, months, and days, are but descriptives and symbolic representations. This figure of 13.8 billion. Sixty to the second and to the hour, or 24 to the day, and 30 to the month. All these are a *Count* of Time. Not Time itself, for it does not have a tangible or material nature, hence it has no quantitative measure. It does not have motion because it does not occupy space, and as such it has no vector, nor speed, nor velocity. It has no distance of travel, nor direction of travel. For some may argue that Time is ever forward in motion, but that remains a matter of perception, and the greatest ordeal is that man's every sense of perception is earthly, because man has only ever known earthly confines with regards to his sense and perception.

What, then, for the sake of argument, is Time?

Well, truthfully, we do not know. Rather we can never know, because a key proponent of Time is that it originates from something called 'Eternity,' which as we have argued is an incomprehensible concept for the being existent in a temporal dimension. And here we acknowledge that the temporality associated with our sensorial perception of it is but one dimension of 'eternity' which determines the sequential progression of occurrence within which is also constituted a 'rate of decay' that determines the biological processes of living things.

Underlying this perception is an inner sense that the Heart realizes, and more often than not, what the Heart senses of Time is always deluded by what the external senses claim of it. Hence the Almighty's question to mankind on the Day of Reckoning as;

$$قَلَ كَمْ لَبِثْتُمْ فِى ٱلْأَرْضِ عَدَدَ سِنِينَ$$

He will say, "How long did you remain in the Ardh, by a count of years" [111]

---

111 Sūrah al-Muʾminūn 23:112

His saying عدد سنين "a count of years" is purely rhetorical. God Almighty has no interest in 'how many' years or how accurate the count. He is not testing the intellect's ability to rationalize the quantity perceived by the senses, rather He is testing the Heart's realization. Driven by sensory perception, man keeps a count of years, which in one aspect is a vital proponent of his rationalization of reality, but in an another aspect, is not the only proponent. In other words, *"tell me by your own suppositions, or instruments of measure, how long do you think you remained?"*

قَالُوا۟ لَبِثْنَا يَوْمًا أَوْ بَعْضَ يَوْمٍ فَسْـَٔلِ ٱلْعَآدِّينَ

They say, "we remained an age, or part of an age. So ask those who have kept count" [112]

This is their delusion, that not only do they not fully comprehend the question, they do not know the answer to it. For one can say "I lived '60 years' or '80 years'" individually, but how can anyone measure human existence in this realm? For one to even give a definite answer of "how long" they would need to know "when it ended" and "when it began" and they cannot know when it began because they do not know when it will end. For one only knows the origination of a thing by examining the final manifestation of it. And no one knows the Final Hour save for Almighty Allāh. Furthermore, how will they determine either when their supposed theories of human existence revolve around notions of "millions of years" of evolution! Their very assumption is false, and no matter how precise they craft their theories and equations, their conclusion will always be false. And so they defer the question to those who do keep whatever count, those who keep a *measure of* time, a *calculation of* time, in clocks and calendars, those who suppose they have a power because they are able to count.

They are those who, under this assumption of measurement, believe they now have the power to alter reality, to make it whatever they envision it to be, and to govern it under their supposed sovereignty where they are the supreme rulers of the world.

---

112 Sūrah al-Mu'minūn 23:113

And thus Almighty Allāh says unto them;

ٱلَّذِى لَهُۥ مُلْكُ ٱلسَّمَٰوَٰتِ وَٱلْأَرْضِ وَلَمْ يَتَّخِذْ وَلَدًا وَلَمْ يَكُن لَّهُۥ شَرِيكٌ فِى ٱلْمُلْكِ وَخَلَقَ كُلَّ شَىْءٍ فَقَدَّرَهُۥ تَقْدِيرًا

He it is to whom belongs the dominion of the Heavens and the Ardh. Never has He had offspring nor a partner in [the sovereignty of] the dominion. And He has created every thing, thus determining it with precision.[113]

This is Almighty Allāh's power قدر, in that He has a full measure تقدير over each thing He has created. The longevity of each thing is known to Him, and so is 'longevity' itself. For He alone knows whence it begins and where it ends. And true power only belongs to the One who not only knows the beginning and end, but is the One who Originates the beginning and Culminates the end. All other 'power' is but an illusion.

إِنَّمَا مَثَلُ ٱلْحَيَوٰةِ ٱلدُّنْيَا كَمَآءٍ أَنزَلْنَٰهُ مِنَ ٱلسَّمَآءِ فَٱخْتَلَطَ بِهِۦ نَبَاتُ ٱلْأَرْضِ مِمَّا يَأْكُلُ ٱلنَّاسُ وَٱلْأَنْعَٰمُ حَتَّىٰٓ إِذَآ أَخَذَتِ ٱلْأَرْضُ زُخْرُفَهَا وَٱزَّيَّنَتْ وَظَنَّ أَهْلُهَآ أَنَّهُمْ قَٰدِرُونَ عَلَيْهَآ أَتَىٰهَآ أَمْرُنَا لَيْلًا أَوْ نَهَارًا فَجَعَلْنَٰهَا حَصِيدًا كَأَن لَّمْ تَغْنَ بِٱلْأَمْسِ ۚ كَذَٰلِكَ نُفَصِّلُ ٱلْءَايَٰتِ لِقَوْمٍ يَتَفَكَّرُونَ

Indeed an example of the life of this world is like water. We send it down from the sky, and thus it is absorbed by the vegetation of the earth. Of it is [cultivated and] consumed by man and livestock. [This cultivation continues] until the earth has taken on an adornment [of the lights symbolizing their progress] and its occupants think [assume] they have full power over it. We send Our Command by night or day, and thus make it a clean-sown [barren] harvest, as if it never flourished the previous day. Thus do We make clear Our Signs for a people who reflect.[114]

---

113 Sūrah al-Furqān 25:2

114 Sūrah Yūnus 10:24

But man assumes, because he cannot see the parameters of his own Will, that just because he was able to measure a thing, he has complete power and control over it. By fabricating an instrument, he seems to think he can measure Time, and this false power leads him to assume he can control Time. This is, of course, a mere theoretical possibility among theoretical possibilities. It is not the control of time, but the assumption and illusion of control. Rather, on the Day of Reckoning, in the Divine Presence where all veils are lifted, where there are no possibilities nor assumptions, where the Absolute Truth is availed, Man has no choice but to admit— *he had no control!* He had no measure. He only thought he did.

And so the Absolute Truth is availed as such;

$$قَلَ إِن لَّبِثْتُمْ إِلَّا قَلِيلًا ۖ لَّوْ أَنَّكُمْ كُنتُمْ تَعْلَمُونَ$$

He will say, "You remained but for a brief period, if but you knew." [115]

Because their assumption of Time is associated with their assumption of Space, which in its linearity is expressed the manifestation of reality as that which occurs syntactically, thus reflected in their speech. They thus assume of 'Eternity' to be an endless 'amount' of time, in the same way as they would assume of 'infinity' as an endless amount of matter in an endless expanse of space.

But Eternity does not mean "a lot of Time" nor an "endless timeline," because Eternity is not a quantifiable thing. Existing within eternity can be a quantity of time and its varied dimensions, which within themselves may be measurable via the references of occurring events. This is why the existence of man in this earthly domain *must* be understood in its temporal bounds, as something that albeit is perceived linearly, is itself limited. Because if they say that Time is a quantity, we would also ask "What is it a quantity of?" to which there is no answer for we do not know what it is *made* of. And if they say that Time is a constituent of Eternity, then we likewise do not know what Eternity is or what it is made

---

115 Sūrah al-Muʾminūn 23:114

of. Hence, in either case, we can neither assume nor conclude that such a thing whose nature is unknown to us can be given any quantitative limits and measures that are of a human projection.

At this juncture I will introduce the most crucial step missed by most knowledge-seekers, that which makes them fall short of whatever they know, or think they know. That which marks the fine line between having Knowledge itself and merely having 'knowledge of' a thing. This of course falls under the epistemological process and it sits between the elements of practice and conviction, and the element of being. Tread carefully here, line by line.

This step falls under the concept of *Ihsān*, which in its essence is an embodiment of spirituality. This embodiment is not easily acquired because you as the being are still bound to your biological form, and there is no separation from that form until the occurrence of death. Even sleep, which offers a partial separation, cannot ensure that embodiment. Successful separation can be achieved by *one* means and it is the *only* means. This means is *knowledge* of a specific kind. The kind that settles in the heart as *Ma'rifah* معرفة. It is the kind that surpasses text and form, surpasses sign and symbol, and further surpasses meaning, to be a kind of *understanding* deep within the heart that, if one tried to express, cannot express or articulate for no aspect of semantic language exists to express that knowledge.

This spiritual understanding places the being in a state that is detached from the causal world, what we would regard as the highest level of intelligence, أدناه ترك الدنيا, when the intellect (and the Heart) has parted from the *Dunya* below and risen, to now examine the realm perspective not of the *Dunya*. What I mean by this is that in order to truly understand something, any 'thing,' one must know it in a reality other than its formal reality. You cannot fully study a building while you are inside it. You cannot study your body while you are inside the body. You cannot study a painting if you are part of the painting.

The paradox of this is that certain aspects of reality simply cannot be detached from. You cannot study your body because you cannot leave it, but you can study *a* body that is not your own to gain an abstract understanding of what *your* body might be. In this literal instant, you are not a part of the form that is being studied. In the same manner that we said, that any 'thing' in the realm cannot explain itself because it is itself, and can only come to an understanding of itself through some conscious reflection of itself.

Consider then, the fish in the water who are oblivious to the state in which they exist. They cannot know the water because they are *in* the water. To them, the medium of their existence is incomprehensible because they are not detached from it. You are a living being, you exist *in* life, and while you may be able to probe the outwardness of life, you can only truly realize its essence when you are detached from it. This is what we mean by our saying that death is what truly unveils the meaning of life, for it is the moment and the medium of detachment from life.

Likewise, we are existent *in* Time. We cannot fully comprehend the reality of Time so long as we are, consciously, submerged in Time. Notions such as 'temporal' and 'eternal' are purely abstract from our sensory perception because the progression of *knowing* through sensoria is itself entwined with Time. Unless the moment unfolds, the senses will be stationary. Nothing new can be known, and nothing of the past can be realized. If suspended in the moment, where the moment itself is stationary, the being remains stationary, and conscious realization of the state of existence also remains stationary. The being can neither affirm nor negate reality because the moment is not unfolding.

In this instance, even the moment itself, albeit stationary, cannot be realized. Either the moment must unfold, or the being must move. If we say that Time is Relative, as is commonly propagated, then Time must be in motion. Thus the being must wait until Time has moved for some progression to be noted in order to affirm or negate the reality of that progression. However, the 'waiting' itself is a proponent of Time, in that for one to 'wait', Time must unfold for a duration of waiting to be realized. This paradoxically negates itself as Time being Relative. We then say that Time is Absolute, in that *it* is not moving, rather the Being is moving. The motion of the being is either in space or in Time. If it is in space, it is also in Time, ergo, the Being is, in either case, in motion through Time. This means that the Being is existent in a medium, and that medium is Time itself.

In realization of this motion, the being must then affirm that he is an entity and Time is an entity. In order to study this latter entity, Time, he must consciously detach himself from the medium of existence, to now examine it objectively, much like the fish who, in order to realize what the water is, must detach from the water.

This poses a conundrum. Did the older fish detach from the water, to exist on land in order to understand the water? No. For the fish cannot exist without the medium of their existence. Realization cannot take place in a state of Timelessness. The detachment here, as we explained above, is a spiritual detachment which is only possible through knowledge. The older fish was a wiser fish, and wisdom comes from knowledge.

Knowledge, in this spiritual state, is of a much higher calibre in that the knowledge itself is not a constituent of forms, symbols, or semantic information. It is an understanding gained from a realization that a much higher form of reality exists, in which one can then consciously affirm that there is a temporality to the lower form of existence and an eternity to the higher form of existence.

Thus does the Almighty say;

وَٱلْعَصْرِ

By (the passage of) Time,

إِنَّ ٱلْإِنسَٰنَ لَفِى خُسْرٍ

Indeed, mankind is in loss,

إِلَّا ٱلَّذِينَ ءَامَنُوا۟ وَعَمِلُوا۟ ٱلصَّٰلِحَٰتِ وَتَوَاصَوْا۟ بِٱلْحَقِّ وَتَوَاصَوْا۟ بِٱلصَّبْرِ

Except for those who believe and do righteous deeds and enjoin each other with truth and enjoin each other with patience.[116]

The word عصر can mean 'age' 'era' 'epoch' or a 'period' that is itself unfolding, not stationary. This does not mean that 'time is relative because it is not stationary' for 'stationary' itself does not mean 'absolute.' The phrase 'motion of time' is an articulation of perception, and its 'motion' is not a displacement of space where it covers a certain distance. Rather the 'motion' is in what it unfolds. It can be likened to a 'river' within

---

116 Sūrah Al-'Asr 103:1-3

which is the flowing water. The river is absolute. It has an ordained course and its prime purpose is to guide the water in that ordained course. The water is perceived as 'moving' but the river does not 'move.' This water is the collection of 'events' and 'occurrences,' each drop of the water in its appropriate place. Each event in Time is likened to the water in the river before it has entered into the cup, or rather the water in the cup is the ordained destiny of each event while it is still in the river. The 'passage' or 'period of time' is the length of the river, and its 'motion' is perceived as how fast or slow the water moves in the river.

In that regard, the human mind cannot rationalize the full measure of the water in the river. He can only rationalize the water in the cup by measuring the cup. The cup is therefore the instrument of measure. The clock that facilitates a count of Time. The cup is not the water, and the water is not the river. Likewise, the clock is not time, and time is not eternity. In relation to the river, Man is but a speck. He was not there when the river was carved. He merely found it there, and realized that from it comes his sustenance. He cannot fully encompass it, for he cannot traverse its entire span in a single grasp. But he can envision it in his mind. He can form an image of it, an abstract concept of how long it might be, from where it begins, and to where it culminates, which he can only do by estimating the capacity of the cup relative to the water it can hold.

In this regard, only the fewest of the few who are gifted passage into the realm of higher and spiritual intelligence, can formulate the most correct understanding of it. Most of mankind is at a loss to comprehend the reality of the medium they exist in, because most of mankind is reliant solely on a sensory rationalization of a medium that itself has no sensory affiliation. You can only see the cup and the water it holds. You can only see a perspective bank of the river and water in that vicinity. You cannot see the entire river nor all the water flowing through it.

Likewise, Time cannot be seen, heard, tasted, smelled, or felt. One may argue that it can be 'sensed' to which we would pose the question 'which sense?' Because the internal senses, which are themselves non-sensory, are also senses. Common Sense, Cognition and Recognition, the Imaginative Faculty, the Estimative Faculty, and Memory and Recollection, which further extend inwards into Abstraction and

Conceptualization. These are the elements that truly 'sense' the effect of Time on the being, and they all relate to intellection as the higher dimension of the 'Soul'. What then, if not belief, that truly refines the soul to a state of purity that enables this higher intellection? And who is the believer if not one with a sound heart قلب سليم ؟

Thus does the Almighty say;

$$يَوْمَ لَا يَنْفَعُ مَالٌ وَلَا بَنُونَ$$

The Day (of Reckoning) when not will benefit [anyone] wealth or offspring (progeny and legacy)

$$إِلَّا مَنْ أَتَى اللَّهَ بِقَلْبٍ سَلِيمٍ$$

Except the one who comes to Allāh with a Sound Heart.[117]

And a sound heart can only be achieved through righteousness, through Truth, and through Patience. He who realizes his *being* and the *Time* in which he exists, will realize that Time is all he has. You are the fish, and the water you exist in is Time. It is the precious medium in which your life unfolds. If you spend it on the world, caught in the river's reeds and weeds, whatever you will acquire in exchange will not benefit your eternal existence. For the river is destined to reach the eternal ocean. If you did not learn to navigate its water, how then will you swim in the depths of the ocean?

---

117 Sūrah Ash-Shu'arā 26:88-89

ACTIONS
AND
INTENTIONS

Causes and Effects are simple enough to collate and comprehend. The nature of our world is causal-effectual. Each thing affects another and is itself affected by another, and an apparent link between each occurrence can be deduced. However, something truly astounding exists as a principle of this causal-effectual relationship in that while the causes and effects can be materially known, the link itself is immaterial.[118] No one can point out the link itself and yet cannot deny its apparent existence. This link is itself non-linear and non-sequential, rather it is a nexus of multiple links, because along with the apparent components of a causal-effectual equation there are also conditions and variables many of which have no materiality.

---

118   In reality, however, no such link exists. One being the effect of another is simply what is assumed of it in the outward sense. The believer affirms that effect of a cause is ordained, and the relation between the cause and effect is unseen, or simply put, immaterial. For Almighty Allāh can remove the effects that a thing is commonly known to cause, just as he removed the effect of heat and harm from the fire that engulfed Nabī Ibrāhim (عليه السلام). If a certain medicine is known to bring relief, the relief being the effect, He Almighty can suspend it, regardless of how strong the medicinal cause, and such phenomenons can be observed and affirmed as true.

For example, I can strike a drum to result in a sound. Here one can say the cause is my hand and the effect is the sound produced. There is no material link between the two, no string or wire of sorts that connects the hand to the drum and the drum to the sound. However, there are a number of conditions and variables that determine the precise effect. My hand must be in the right position, the force exerted can vary in that the strength of my arm or hand will determine how loud the sound. The environment itself will also determine the effect, for instance, if the room is small and soundproofed as opposed to a large open auditorium. Even the components themselves, hand and drum, must exist in that specific time and space to produce that effect. If the hand is there, but the drum is not, there will not be a sound, and likewise.

Consider, then, one's actions and their manifestations. The action performed by the being is the cause to which the effect is the manifestation of the action. The outcome will always vary depending on how the action is performed and which conditions enable which manifestations. One can prepare food to the manifestation of nutrition, but the same preparation may result in illness. The manifestation may be viewed as a tragedy and the action thus condemned, and yet that illness may be the result of a series of other manifestations that would themselves be fruitful. To the effect of that illness, one may visit the doctor, who in his treatment may discover a deeper more harmful ailment unrelated to the food, the early rectification of which may save one's life.

Consider the following parable;

> In a small village lived a man and his only son whom he loved dearly. The boy was kind, charismatic, and respectful. Deep in his heart, the man intended never to be parted from his beloved. Together they bought a beautiful horse, and the people said, "What a blessing," and the man said, "Perhaps." They put the horse to work and earned their livelihood by carting merchandise for the villagers. More often than not, they had loads that were too heavy for the horse, such that one day the horse died of exhaustion. The people offered their condolences saying, "What a tragedy." He said, "Perhaps." He took the corpse away to bury it in the woods. Here he found several wild horses, and he brought them home. The

128

people said, "What a blessing." To that the man said, "Perhaps." His son took a liking to one of the horses, and mounted it, only to be thrown off and break his leg. The people said, "What a tragedy." The man said, "Perhaps." Then came the sultan's agents, seeking to recruit young boys into the army for war. But because of his broken leg, the man's son was not recruited.

Note how the causes and effects are apparent. How each action led to a manifestation, which itself led to another, and that to another, each one seemingly good or bad. One may infer the links between each cause to effect, but they are all manifested upon certain conditions and variables. Had the loads not been heavy, the horse would not have died. Had it not died, the man would not have gone to the woodlands, to which he would not have found the wild horses. Or even if the horse died, but he chose not to bury it in the woods. Or even if the horse did not die, but he chose to go to the woods anyway. The finding of wild horses was contingent on the precise conditions and variables, even the precise Time, for if he had gone to the woods earlier or later, he may not have found the wild horses. To which his son would not have ridden one and broken his leg, to which he may have been parted from his father to join the army, and perhaps even perish in the war. Even so, he may have ridden the horse but not broken his leg, and come the sultan's soldiers, the boy would have been parted from his father.

It would therefore be foolish to dismiss all the peripheral occurrences as things that just "happened-to-be" there to result in those outcomes. These are all means to an end, and if there is an end, there must be a beginning. That beginning cannot be a casual input, for itself would be the effect of a preceding cause to an endless regression and hence would not be a beginning.

Here you must understand that the essential beginning of all causes is immaterial and not of the realm of causes and effects. Consider the creation of the world. In the regression of *all* cosmic events, micro and macro, there is a contingency to the prime cause or initial cause, which cannot originate itself. It is, by necessity, the origination of an issuance. A command, that comes from *outside* the causal realm. This is what we refer to as *'Alam al-Amr* عالم الأمر, and this is the realm in which the command, the order, the will, and the intention originate from. It is an immaterial realm, hence these are all immaterial entities.

In the above parable, the final outcome was not a product of the causes and effects that led to it. It was a result of the intention that superseded them all. All the causes and effects were mere instruments or facilitations, *means* أسباب to manifest that intention. For the man's intention was that he should not be parted from his son, and thus whatever happened was to the manifestation of that intention. To him was what he intended, in that what the people perceived as a tragedy was in reality a blessing, and what they perceived as bounty was not of benefit, for did they not know the final manifestation of all those occurrences, for they did not know the unseen intention of the man.

Thus does the Almighty say;

$$وَعَسَىٰٓ أَن تَكْرَهُواْ شَيْئًا وَهُوَ خَيْرٌ لَّكُمْ ۖ وَعَسَىٰٓ أَن تُحِبُّواْ شَيْئًا وَهُوَ شَرٌّ لَّكُمْ ۗ$$
$$وَٱللَّهُ يَعْلَمُ وَأَنتُمْ لَا تَعْلَمُونَ$$

And it may be that you despise a thing and it is beneficial for you, or it may be that you love a thing and it is ruinous for you. And Allāh knows, and you do not know.[119]

Hence you may intend a thing, but what manifests is not to your liking. How do you know where the ultimate manifestation lies? The man in the parable intended that he no be parted from his son, so that even when they received many horses in bounty, he said *"Perhaps* it is a blessing"* and when his son was injured, he said, *"Perhaps* it is a tragedy."* It was not his place to question what was happening in the unseen reality, but it was his responsibility to work towards keeping his son well. Hence he bought a horse, and worked hard to put food on the table, and affirmed a sound belief and trust that the Almighty will aid him in fulfilling his intention. And all this goes to prove that ultimately, actions and manifestations are contingent on the intentions. This is the deep metaphysical meaning, the wisdom in the Holy Prophet's words (ﷺ);

---

119 Sūrah Al-Baqarah 2:216

إِنَّمَا الْأَعْمَالُ بِالنِّيَّاتِ

Actions are contingent on the Intentions

وَإِنَّمَا لِكُلِّ امْرِئٍ مَا نَوَى

And indeed to each will be what they intended

فَمَنْ كَانَتْ هِجْرَتُهُ إِلَى اللَّهِ وَرَسُولِهِ فَهِجْرَتُهُ إِلَى اللَّهِ وَرَسُولِهِ

So whosoever migrated to Allāh and His messenger, he thus migrated to Allāh and His messenger

وَمَنْ كَانَتْ هِجْرَتُهُ لِدُنْيَا يُصِيبُهَا أَوْ امْرَأَةٍ يَنْكِحُهَا فَهِجْرَتُهُ إِلَى مَا هَاجَرَ إِلَيْهِ

And whosoever migrated to a worldly cause or to take a woman in marriage, he thus migrated to whatever he migrated[120]

It is not as complicated a matter to understand. Whatever one does in terms of the action performed, conscious or autonomous, has a contingency to an intention which is executed by the Will. The action itself, insofar as its quantitativeness, is much less a value if the intention was not true to begin with. The sincerity with which it was intended bears all the significance, for it is initiated by the being in the innermost sanctity of the crucible. We have already established that the responsibility is upon the heart, the contentment is upon the heart, and so is the damnation. If the heart's intent is not honest and sincere to begin with, surely one cannot expect wonders to manifest in the world for them.

The Prophet's saying فَمَنْ كَانَتْ هِجْرَتُهُ إِلَى اللَّهِ وَرَسُولِهِ فَهِجْرَتُهُ إِلَى اللَّهِ وَرَسُولِهِ is a conditional sentence, what is known in Arabic as a جملة شرطية a 'conditional clause,' where the condition and that which is conditioned uses the same terms to elaborate that one manifests what they intend. Which is to say if you sow a good seed, you will reap a good fruit. In this example, whoever intended to do for Allāh and His messenger, then that is what they did. This has been given a higher rank than the statement that follows. Whoever intended to do for worldly aspects, wealth مَالٌ, or for relationship, progeny and legacy بَنُونَ, then that is what they did it for. This must be understood in the Arabic language to fully appreciate the articulated rhetoric. It infers in this latter statement that the intent

---

120 متفق عليه in all the books of Hadīth

131

related to anything other than the Divine is not even worth repeating, and if closely examined, both the aforementioned are also exemplified in the Āyāt we spoke of at the end of the previous chapter;

$$يَوْمَ لَا يَنْفَعُ مَالٌ وَلَا بَنُونَ$$

The Day (of Reckoning) when not will benefit [anyone] wealth or offspring (progeny and legacy)

$$إِلَّا مَنْ أَتَى اللَّهَ بِقَلْبٍ سَلِيمٍ$$

Expect the one who comes to Allāh with a Sound Heart.[121]

Every one will have what they intended, لِكُلِّ امْرِئٍ مَا نَوَى, meaning everyone will manifest what they intend. Meaning the manifestation of what occurs in the physical material realm is contingent on that which occurs in the metaphysical. The خلق *Khalq* is contingent on the أمر *Amr*. The ملك *Mulk* is contingent on the ملكوت *Malakūt*. The Body is contingent on the Soul. The Soul is contingent on the Heart. The Heart is contingent on the Being. If the being does not exist, the heart cannot exist. If the heart does not exist, the soul has no purpose. If there is no soul, the body has no use. What happens internally will manifest externally, and if the internal conditions change, the external conditions will correspondingly change.

While most in modernity are compulsively obsessed with the cultivation of their body and bodily aspects, of this outward world of theirs and all its material glory, you, my dear reader, should do the opposite. Cultivating the body does not perfect the soul. Rather, cultivating the Soul perfects the body. And purifying the Heart perfects the Soul. And if you should place deep within your heart this seed of Honesty and Sincerity, and turn your inner gaze towards the seeking of your Lord's Presence then you will achieve success both internally and externally.

This you can only achieve through knowledge. True Knowledge. Praiseworthy Knowledge. For to *Know* your Lord, you must know that which is attributed to Him. His Signs. His Speech. That which He has

---

121 Sūrah Ash-Shu'arā 26:88-89

revealed. And to know His signs, you must study the Signs. To achieve this, you must dedicate your existence to that action of learning and studying. For it is through this that you will know how to formulate your intention, and how your will should be executed. How you will distinguish between right and wrong, if you do not *know* what is right and do not *know* what is wrong?

The Holy Prophet (ﷺ) also said;

قَالَ إِنَّمَا الدُّنْيَا لِأَرْبَعَةِ نَفَرٍ

عَبْدٍ رَزَقَهُ اللَّهُ مَالاً وَعِلْمًا فَهُوَ يَتَّقِي فِيهِ رَبَّهُ وَيَصِلُ فِيهِ رَحِمَهُ وَيَعْلَمُ لِلَّهِ فِيهِ حَقًّا

فَهَذَا بِأَفْضَلِ الْمَنَازِلِ

وَعَبْدٍ رَزَقَهُ اللَّهُ عِلْمًا وَلَمْ يَرْزُقْهُ مَالاً فَهُوَ صَادِقُ النِّيَّةِ يَقُولُ لَوْ أَنَّ لِي مَالاً لَعَمِلْتُ بِعَمَلِ فُلَانٍ

فَهُوَ بِنِيَّتِهِ فَأَجْرُهُمَا سَوَاءٌ

وَعَبْدٍ رَزَقَهُ اللَّهُ مَالاً وَلَمْ يَرْزُقْهُ عِلْمًا فَهُوَ يَخْبِطُ فِي مَالِهِ بِغَيْرِ عِلْمٍ لاَ يَتَّقِي فِيهِ رَبَّهُ وَلاَ يَصِلُ فِيهِ رَحِمَهُ وَلاَ يَعْلَمُ لِلَّهِ فِيهِ حَقًّا

فَهَذَا بِأَخْبَثِ الْمَنَازِلِ

وَعَبْدٍ لَمْ يَرْزُقْهُ اللَّهُ مَالاً وَلاَ عِلْمًا فَهُوَ يَقُولُ لَوْ أَنَّ لِي مَالاً لَعَمِلْتُ فِيهِ بِعَمَلِ فُلَانٍ

فَهُوَ بِنِيَّتِهِ فَوِزْرُهُمَا سَوَاءٌ

The world is only for four persons:

A slave, whom Allāh provides wealth and knowledge, and he has trust in his Lord, and he nurtures the ties of kinship, and he knows that Allāh has a right in it.

This is the most virtuous rank.

And a slave whom Allāh provides knowledge but does not provide wealth. So he has a truthful intent, saying: 'If I had wealth, then I would do the deeds of so-and-so with it.'

By his intention, their rewards are the same.

And a slave whom Allāh provides wealth but does not provide knowledge. So he spends his wealth [aimlessly] without knowledge, nor does he have trust in his Lord, nor does he nurture the ties of kinship, nor does he know that Allāh has a right in it.

This is the most despicable rank.

And a slave whom Allāh does not provide with wealth nor knowledge, so he says: 'If I had wealth, then I would do the deeds of so-and-so with it.'

By his intention, their sins are the same.[122]

Of the first kind, his wealth and its spending (the action and its manifestation) are sound and righteous, because the execution of his will is guided by wisdom which is guided by the knowledge he has been given. The gifts themselves, of knowledge and wealth, do not determine his righteous station, rather it is the intention by which he then uses them that truly define his piety. He has the intention to seek knowledge and to acquire wealth, both with the intention to spend them in servitude of his Lord. Thus does Allāh give him wealth and knowledge by giving him the means to acquire them.

Of the second kind, who has knowledge, but no wealth, he is likened to the first because he is cognizant that both knowledge and wealth come from Allāh. He is grateful for the one he has and patient for the one he does not, and as such he places the intention in his heart, that if at all his Lord was to bestow it to him, the wealth being the means by which he could amplify how much right he could do, then he would do it.

Of these two kinds, their reward is equal. Because their intentions are equal. For both have manifested in their hearts *Trust* تقوى in their Lord, and are cognizant of their responsibilities, and the Right of their Lord over their affairs and their kin.

Of the third kind, albeit wealthy, has no knowledge, and so his wealth is squandered. He does not realize that the wealth he has came from his Lord, and so does not know the true value of what he has, nor realize its responsibility upon him. For the test of wealth is two-fold. To whomever it is given is the test of sharing, and we see this in the first kind. To whomever it is not given is the test of patience, and we see this

---

122 Jamī at-Tirmīdhī 2325

in the second kind. Of any other kind, because the very intention in their hearts are selfish, their rank is the most despicable and immoral rank.

Of the forth kind, who has no knowledge nor wealth, is the kind who remains deluded in wishful thinking. He says, wishfully, that if he had wealth, he would spend it wisely and responsibly, but without the knowledge to aid him, the intention has no conviction. For we affirm, that Faith without Knowledge is ignorance.

Of these two kinds, the resultant sin of their actions or inactions are equal. Because their intentions are equal. Either selfish or wishful. Without knowledge, they do not know who they are, what their purpose is, and to whom they owe their allegiance. They are not cognizant of their responsibilities and duties, nor the Right of their Lord over their affairs and their kin.

The focus of the Hadīth is on the second and forth kind, who are likened to the first and third kind respectively. One who has knowledge but no wealth is likened to one who has both and is righteous. He only lacks the means. But because his intention is sincere, his outward manifestation is righteous. The other who has no knowledge or wealth is likened to one who has wealth but no knowledge. For without knowledge he is ignorant, and his ignorance plants a diseased intention, such that his outward manifestation is despicable.

In both cases, knowledge lies at the seed of it all. For if one does not see food, he does not eat, as he does not *know* it is there. And if he sees food, he still may not eat it if the will to do it is not there. And even if he wills it, he still may not eat it if the means to reach it are not there. The action, being the eating of food, is contingent on the means to acquire it. The means to acquire it are contingent on the will to seek out the means. And the will to seek out the means is contingent on the knowledge of executing the will. For the being to fully realize the manifestation of his intention, all three must be there; *Knowledge*, followed by the *Will*, which is followed by the *Means*. Hence the primary pursuit of the being is to seek knowledge, which itself is contingent on the *intention* to seek knowledge.

But here is the conundrum. You have a defined duration of existence, within which is contained an array of necessary activities that must be performed to the fulfillment of your existence. In the time that you have,

135

you cannot possibly accomplish everything you intend, particularly not if you are unable to distinguish between the intent of your carnal self and the intent of your heart. You are existent in a realm of causes and effects, happenings and phenomena. There are things that draw your attention. Things that distract you. Things that keep you occupied until your time runs out. And as we elaborated in the previous chapter, the only way to truly realize the medium you exist in, which is Time, is through spiritual detachment from the material realm. And this is achieved through *Ihsān* إحسان.

Perhaps now we can understand the Holy Prophet's (ﷺ) wisdom when he said;

مِنْ حُسْنِ إِسْلَامِ الْمَرْءِ تَرْكُهُ مَا لَا يَعْنِيهِ

From the spiritual beauty of one's submission is to leave that which does not concern him.[123]

Ihsān is to detach from the causes and effects. The happenings. The occurrences. Ihsān is to leave that which does not concern you. This material realm does not concern you. The spiritual realm concerns you. The hereafter concerns you. Concern yourself with *that*, not *this*. So you can allocate your precious Time in the pursuit of *knowing* that which is worthy of knowing, *enroute* of which you may adhere to the path that will take you to the Divine Presence where you will find an everlasting contentment, thus leaving behind all that is petty and trivial and frivolous.

---

123 Muwatta Mālik 1638, Jamī at-Tirmīdhī 2317, and Sunan Ibn Mājah 3967

SPIRITUAL
ASCENSION

Man's destination at the time of his creation was to the lowest of the low. The earthly, material realm. What do we expect as a response when we ask if this was the final destination? For it could be argued that if it was to be his final destination, then everything that Man is presently doing, in all his exploitations as geared towards his envisioned utopia of an engineered paradise, is all justified. If it is not so, then where indeed is his destination?

Logically, if he is in the lowest of the low, the destination can only be the highest of the high. If his present state is material, his ascent can only be spiritual.

Arguable, the most challenging thought in our contemporary age is centered around the ethics of science and technology. A technology is that which is crafted, and as such has a purpose to fulfill as intended by the craftsman. What is that purpose? Or rather, should we ask, what is the purpose of technology?

If it is to bring comfort and leisure, whyever should man seek to leave this realm and ascend elsewhere, since the elsewhere, as Paradise, has but one purpose and that is to bring leisure and comfort. Is there a need for that then if the technology can fulfill it here? If this is justifiable, then its science is also justifiable, and whatever is ethically debated can easily be resolved as 'doing for the greater good.'

The resultant world-view is one that suggests a parting from abstinence of that which satisfies carnal pleasures, to in turn indulge in those carnal pleasures. As what is deduced from an 'ideal' paradise is fulfillment of said pleasures. Since the paradise is being engineered in this material medium, one sees no reason to abstain from them. The materially designed utopian world-view does not place an obligation on the being to restrain from indulgence if they have the means to attain them. For that, Man has created something called 'capitalism' giving each individual an 'equal' chance to opportune whatever enterprise that would fulfill, and perchance exceed the means. Likewise, there is no obligation to act and react per one's volition however they so choose, in 'defense' of their opinions or in preemptively attacking to preserve their self or foreign interests. For that, they have created 'Freedom of Speech' and given it platforms called 'Social Media.' Hence anyone can act or react however they so will, to quench whatever it is of human nature that needs quenching, all so long as no arbitrary 'laws,' set by the same institutions that are cultivating this engineered paradise, are broken.

That is *Secularism*. A crown of frail paper worn by the foolish and the ignoramus, who has, by his own convoluted notions, come to the conclusion that there is no reality beyond his material and biological reality. Through epochs of 'evolution,' Man has become 'intelligent,' and his intelligence, or the lack thereof, tells him that this life is pointless and meaningless. So enjoy, celebrate, indulge, and satisfy. You only live once, after all!

There is no word in the tongues of Man, Angels, and Jinn, for the height of this stupidity. For if man is a mere biological entity, meaningless and insignificant in this realm, any pursuit of comfort and leisure is equally pointless and meaningless. If man is only a biological being, any purpose of life and existence is likewise pointless. Thus argues the athiest, nihilist, and agnostic, all under the banner of secularism.

We, however, say that man is not just a biological entity, and that his heart is spiritually eternal, and if at all man should ascend, it is his heart that will ascend. And in order to ascend, he must build a ladder with which to ascend. And to climb this ladder, he must lighten himself of those carnal pleasures that weigh him down. He must cultivate this terminal state of existence in such a way as to facilitate that ascent.

And for that purpose, the heart has been given troops. Skilled soldiers who, if properly and strategically directed, will strive on its behalf to conquer its carnal existence and rise an honored being.

I will not claim to be enlightened in this matter, nor a master of my own 'self.' For I am equally a struggling servant, and perhaps the best person to elaborate this to you is one who has striven this path and mastered it himself, Imam AbūHāmid Al-Ghazzālī. This follows from his treatise, كيمياء السعادة *The Alchemy of Happiness.* And I will take you through these sections step by step;

[I have placed the Arabic text in segments followed by my own translation, and my commentary and explanation of each section is in the footnotes]

فصل في معرفة القلب وعسكره
On knowing the Heart and its Troops

اعلم أنه قيل في المثل المشهور
Know then, that it has been said in a renowned allegory:[124]

إن النفس كالمدينة، واليدين والقدمين وجميع الأعضاء ضياعها
Indeed the soul is like the City, and the hands, legs, and all the extensions of the body, are its farms and villages,[125]

---

124 The origin of this allegory is not known, but its wisdom is an essential blueprint in humanity. As we mentioned in the first chapter, the human being is a reflection of the cosmos, and the cosmos is a reflection of the human being. The essential mode of cosmological governance is also embodied in man's own governance, and this allegory proves that governance, as is applied, regardless of the particulars of application, has a universal blueprint. Your task here is to understand the universality of this allegory in relation to your Heart and how it governs your being. Each component is likened to that which is evident in governance, and you as the "being" are ever in a mode of governing your "self."

125 The farms and villages fall into the legislation of the city. Likewise, your body and all its extensions are governed by your soul. We said that the soul enlivens the body. The body is existent because the soul exists, in much the same way that farms and villages surround the city because the city exists. The city does not exist because the farms and villages exist, likewise the soul does not exist because the body exists.

والقوة الشهوانية واليها

And the concupiscent faculty is like its Administration [126]

والقوة الغضبية شحنتها

And the Irascible faculty is like the Defense Force.[127]

والقلب ملكها

And the Heart is their King.[128]

والعقل وزيرها

And the Intellect is its (the Heart's) Vizier.[129]

والملك يدبرهم حتى تستقر مملكته وأحواله؛

And the King manages them until his kingdom and its states are stable.[130]

---

126 The literal translation would be "Governor", but I am using contemporarily familiar terms to facilitate a better understanding. Included in my rendering of the term "Administration" is the "Governor" and the "Politician". You will understand as we progress why I have translated it as such.

127 Likewise, the literal translation would be "Police", but I have used "Defense Force" to include "Police" as well as "Military" and "Law Enforcement."

128 The dynamic of this type of governance is fundamental. It is the only type of governance known to man, regardless of the system (monarchic, aristocratic, republic, democratic, or whatever) and regardless of the terms used to denote these three faculties. The administration is responsible for state and municipal matters. The police and military is responsible for internal law enforcement and external defense. The Vizier's department, which includes legislation, is responsible for establishing justice and order across the board.

129 Think of the Vizier as a "Prime Minister" the one place in charge of overseeing the administration and defense of the kingdom.

130 The English language is deficient in its expressive ability. The term يدبر carries the meaning of "manage" but also carries the meaning of "turning back" or "reflects upon" as a manner of examining and analyzing to maintain sound governance and rectify anything that disrupts that governance. The contemporary meaning of 'management' is often projected as progressive in a forward-linear fashion, but in reality it is progressive in a back-and-forth mode. The strength and value of true leadership has the outward issuance of directive, which is only sound when there is an inward dynamic of self-rectification. Hence the true 'Khalīfah' as exemplified by Ādam is one who is *responsible* for his actions.

لأن الوالي - وهو الشهوة - كذاب فضولي مخلط

Because the Administration, which is the Concupiscent Faculty, is a liar, meddlesome, and confused.[131]

والشحنة - وهو الغضب - شرير قتال خراب

And the Defense Force, which is the Irascible Faculty, is hostile, violent, and destructive. [132]

---

131 Ghazzālī's choice of words here is truly intellectual. He is designating the base nature of governors and politicians as being liars, meddlesome, and confused, foremost because politics is a subjective field where facts can be true, but those facts can equally be manipulated to be false which is the nature of lying. The field of politics is not inherently an intellectual field, but intelligence can be applied to condition and nurture the field. Secondly, politicians and governors are constitutionally bureaucratic, solely concerned with following set procedures, outside of which whatever intelligence they have is predisposed and preoccupied in overriding and competing with each other, which results in them concerning themselves more with each other's affairs than doing what needs to be done. It means that they are selfish, not selfless, as likened to the soul that either become 'self'-*less* or remain 'self'-*ish*. This is the nature of a bureaucratic mindset, where it is taken for granted that whatever system is in place will function autonomously so long as that system satisfies the administration. Ibn Khaldūn rendered a government as الحكومة مؤسسة تمنع الظلم بخلاف ما ترتكبه "*an institution that will prevent injustice other than what it itself commits.*" To those whose governance is natively flawed, it does not matter if the system brings justice to the people, so long as they are pleased with it operating in their favor. The natural result of "lying" and "meddling" is being in a state of confusion. Politics being a purely semantic field, it is ever changing and shifting. My conviction has always been that so long as one is caught up in the semantics and particulars, stagnating in the political landscape, they will always be in a state of confusion, where what might be true now, becomes false later, or what might be false now becomes true later. Regardless of all that, these may be entities that cannot think for themselves, but they are not alienated from guidance, rather they flourish and contribute to the wellbeing of the state when they are guided and nurtured, and will likewise cause ruination when left to their own volitions.

132 Likewise, the very nature of the police and military is hostile in the sense of assuming every occurrence to be a threat. Such a nature is *always* reactionary, and the only reaction to a threat is violence. The natural result of hostility and violence is always destructive. And just like the politicians and governors, the military arm is not a self-reflective or intellective entity. The soldier is trained to follow order and procedure, not to think. If the nation's governance is left to the military, its people cannot be expected to flourish. Which is why 'martial law' is only ever instituted in states of emergency. It cannot be the normative form of governance.

141

فإن تركهم الملك على ما هم عليه، هلكت المدينة وخربت؛ فيجب أن يشاور الملك

الوزير، ويجعل الوالي والشحنة تحت يد الوزير. فإذا فعل ذلك استقرت أحوال

المملكة وتعمرت المدينة

So if the King allows them to operate on their own accord, the City will be destroyed and ruined. (In this regard) it is important that the King counsels with his Vizier. And he places the Administration and the Defense Force under the control of the Vizier. If he does that, the states of the Kingdom will be stable, and the City will flourish and prosper.[133]

وكذلك القلب يشاور العقل

And likewise (as in the allegory) the Heart counsels the Intellect,[134]

ويجعل الشهوة والغضب تحت حكمه، حتى تستقر أحوال النفس

and places the Concupiscent Faculty and the Irascible Faculty under its control, until the Psychological States are stabilized,[135]

---

133 Because sound governance requires sound intellection, and true leadership is delegative not dictatorial. Which is to say that the leader does not attempt to control every decision, but that he regulates delegating governance to a designated thinker. This designated thinker is the overseer, or the Vizier, or Prime Minister, who is capable of resolving the issues encountered by his administration and defense force.

134 Or the Mind/Rational Faculty, which is a component of the Soul. Since only the Intellect is capable of intellection, it has been ordained to be the 'thinker'. The Heart being the Sultan must then consult the intellect over the concupiscent and irascible faculties, for the intellect is capable of rational action. The other two are reactionary.

135 'Psychological States' أحوال النفس is a technical term. There is no one defaulted psychological state that could be defined as "normal" often propagated by secular so-called psychology. "Normal" in Islām is not a set quantity. It is a dynamic spectrum, since every Soul has its own burdens, tests, and circumstances. Each Soul's state is also affected by its environs, both geographical and societal. What maybe "normal" for one is not the same for another. Likewise, each "normal" state changes in life. The parameters of "normalcy" are defined by religious boundaries, not political or societal norms. All the states have their recommended levels of normalcy, which are Islamically defined as when they are harmonious within the being, which are in turn considered normal when they are functioning within ordained parameters.

ويصل إلى سبب السعادة من معرفة الحضرة الإلهية

and it (the Heart) arrives at the means of felicity and contentment from an understanding of the Divine Presence. [136]

ولو جعل العقل تحت يد الغضب والشهوة، هلكت نفسه، وكان قلبه شقيا في الآخرة

But if it places the Intellect beneath the control of the Irascible and Concupiscent Faculties, the Soul will be destroyed, and the Heart will be damned in the HereAfter (eternally).

فصل وظيفة القلب
On the Virtue of the Heart

اعلم أن الشهوة والغضب خادمان للنفس

Know then that the Irascible faculty and the Concupiscent faculty are 'fetching servants' of the soul.[137]

جاذبان يحفظان أمر الطعام والشراب والنكاح لعمل الحواس

They preserve the affairs of eating, drinking, and copulation, to the service of the senses.[138]

---

136 The term معرفة here denotes a kind of 'knowing' we would define as an *'innermost understanding'* as opposed to a knowing of 'scientia' or علم. This latter term of علم that is acquired through 'learning' is used in reference to 'intellection' or the 'Knowing *of*' which pertains terms, definitions, facts, equations, symbols and such. The knowledge of معرفة is done by the Heart as an *understanding*, and this understanding cannot be quantified or defined. Another such term which will be used later is إدراك 'realization,' which is also done by the Heart, and is a term frequently used in the Qurān.

137 The way to rationalize this is to imagine the soul having two dimensions. On the one side is the Intellect with the Heart, and this side is linked to the *Ru'h* روح. The other side, which is the 'lower' dimension, includes the Concupiscent and Irascible faculties, which are linked to the *Body* جسم. These two are constantly shifting between the body and the Intellect. They 'fetch' the requirements of the body and relay them to the Intellect. The intellect may intuitively fulfill these requirements or may require the Heart's decision.

138 Not limited to the commonly known five senses of sight, sound, taste, smell, and touch. Every component of the body is essentially a sense. The five are called Perceptive Senses, the rest may be called Receptive Senses.

143

ثم النفس خادم الحواس شبكة العقل وجواسيسه

Thus does the soul serve the senses (by acting) as a net for the Intellect and its 'spies.' [139]

يبصر بها صنائع البارئ جلت قدرته

It is with these (senses or 'spies') that it (the intellect) sees the forms that the Almighty, Exalted be He, has created. [140]

ثم الحواس خادم العقل

Thus do the senses serve the Intellect. [141]

وهو للقلب سراج وشمعة يبصر بنوره الحضرة الإلهية

And it is to the Heart a lamp and a candle that with its light it (the Heart) can see the Divine Presence. [142]

لأن الجنة وهي نصيب الجوف أو الفرج محتقرة في جنب تلك الجنة

For the paradise in which the stomach and genitals delight pales in comparison to that 'other' paradise. [143]

---

139 All the information acquired through the senses reaches the Soul first via what is known as the 'Breast' or 'Chest' صدر. This likened to what is allegorically called the 'Niche' مشكاة as we discussed in Chapter Six - *The Lamp and its Light.* It is the cavity through which all the sensory information, after it has been processed by the brain, passes to reach the Intellect.

140 The Intellect, ergo, the Soul and Heart, cannot access the material realm of the body except through the senses. If the senses are cut off, the being cannot perceive the realm of created forms.

141 The senses continually probe the outer world for information to the demand of the Intellect. We say that the Intellect cannot be idle. It is ever active in the interpretation of symbols, whether the being is awake or asleep. In the sleep state, the being is in a realm of symbols عالم المثال, where the senses are not needed. In the wakeful state, the being is the realm of the body عالم التراب, and the prime source of information comes from the senses.

142 The intellect does not deal with the Forms that are perceived. Rather what it does is associate symbols to the Forms, and to further interpret the symbols by associating them to meanings.

143 Meaning the delight of sensory satisfaction is temporal to the delight of spiritual contentment, and since the heart is a spiritual entity, its true contentment does not lie in sensory delights of the stomach and genitals. Because it *knows* (as an inherent knowing) that it was destined for eternity, not temporality, and that the enjoyment of this realm is temporal, but the contentment of the Paradise is eternal.

ثم العقل خادم القلب

Thus does the Intellect serve the Heart.[144]

والقلب مخلوق لنظر جمال الحضرة الإلهية

And the Heart was created but to see the Beauty of the Divine Presence. [145]

---

144 The Heart, being of the Essential Realm عالم الأمر, is ultimately able to comprehend through the meanings that the Intellect interprets from Symbols and Forms of the Created Realm عالم الخلق. If the intellect is not properly trained to associate the forms to their symbols, or to properly interpret the symbols, the heart will receive inaccurate meanings, and their being's perception of the world will be false. The association of Form to Symbol and Meaning is the essential blueprint of language, since language is the institution of symbols and meanings. If the language is deficient, the being's understanding will be deficient. Likewise, the being's perception, or world-view, is entirely dependent on the language used. In simpler terms, the Senses perceive Forms, the Intellect interprets Symbols, and the Heart comprehends Meanings. All three must be harmonious with the Truth for the being to be harmonious with Reality.

145 This is the ultimate purpose of Knowledge and the Heart's purpose of seeking it. The collected information from the sensory world, the symbols collated in language, the interpretations done by the Intellect, are all directed towards the Heart's knowing and comprehending, and all its knowledge is purposed towards knowing the Divine Presence. This is the litmus test of any probing of information or acquisition of knowledge. If it does not, or seems not to lead to the Divine Presence, it is not Praiseworthy Knowledge, and thus cannot even be called 'Knowledge.' For only that which leads one to knowing their Lord can truly be worthy of the word 'Knowledge,' and it is itself of an immaterial nature for it settles only in the Heart and no place else. This is why we make the distinction between 'Knowledge' and 'Information' and thus should the being make the distinction between what he truly knows and what he *thinks* he knows. Mastering a science, or memorizing an entire text, having the ability to recall various narrations, opinions, or citations does not mean one has knowledge. It could only be said that they have 'knowledge of' things, meaning information, but not having knowledge itself. If whatever one learns does not foremost penetrate the Heart, following which does not enable the Heart to see the Divine Presence in all things and happenings, it cannot be called 'Knowledge.' The being may flaunt however many degrees, qualifications, and accreditations they have, none of these will bear any value on the Day of Reckoning as a mark of piety. Imam Mālik said, ليس العلم بكثرة الروايات لكن العلم نور يضع الله في قلب المؤمن, *Knowledge is not an abundance of opinions, facts, and narrations, rather Knowledge is a Light that Allāh places in the Heart of the Believer.*

فمن اجتهد في هذه الصنعة، فهو عبد حق، من غلمان الحضرة

So he who strives in this craftsmanship, such is the True
Servant, from the youthfulness of that presence.[146]

كما قال سبحانه وتعالى: وَمَا خَلَقْتُ ٱلْجِنَّ وَٱلْإِنسَ إِلَّا لِيَعْبُدُونِ

As He, Glorified be He, has said, "And not did I create the
Jinn and the Man, but that they would serve Me"[147]

معناه: إنا خلقنا القلب، وأعطيناه الملك والعسكر، وجعلنا النفس مركبة، حتى يسافر
عليه من عالم التراب إلى أعلى عليين.

It means: We created the Heart, and We gave it troops and
a dominion, and We placed the soul as its vessel, so that it can
journey upon it from the realm of matter, to the highest of the
high.[148]

---

146 'Craftsmanship' of continually regulating and governing his
'self' to the purpose of 'being' and 'becoming'. In other words,
regardless of the being's worldly occupation, he remains active with
defining his being to the ambition of returning to his Lord in a
state of purity and righteousness. This 'youthfulness' من غلمان الحضرة
is expressed in Al-A'rāf 7:172 as the 'earliest' state of existence for
the human being when he was in the Divine Presence, a state of
pure innocence and highest intellection. In that regard, the concept
of رجع, or 'Return' to the Divine Presence is to be in the best
form and state, this youthful form of purity in which the being
has manifested حسن and has fulfilled the very purpose of his true
nature فطرة.

147 Sūrah Adh-Dhāriyah 51:57, Regarding that Āyah, Ibn Abbās,
Mujāhid, and Ibn Jurayj said إِلَّا لِيَعْرِفُونِ, 'except but to *know.*' That
what is signified by the Āyah, as Ghazzālī elaborates, is the inherent
purpose for which these entities were created. However, the Āyah
does not say that these entities were created in an inherent state of
knowing, which means that their natures were created in such a
way as to choose whether or not they wanted to know their Lord,
by which they would serve their Lord. The term إِلَّا لِيَعْبُدُونِ is the
conclusive result, or the final 'becoming' of the being that is itself
initiated by إِلَّا لِيَعْرِفُونِ, which is to say that in order for the being to
fulfill its purpose of *serving* its Lord, it must first *know* its Lord.

148 This is what Ghazzālī renders as the purpose of the being
relative to the purpose of his peripheral aspects. The body and all
of its faculties along with the soul and all of its faculties, have been
designed to assist the Heart in fulfilling its purpose, by which the
being can fulfill *his* purpose, which is to rise from the temporal
materiality lowest of the low to the spiritual eternity of the highest
of the high. In this, he is probing you to realize your humanity, and
for what destiny that humanity was created.

فإذا أراد أن يؤدي حق هذه النعمة

So if it wants to fulfill its right to this favor,[149]

جلس مثل السلطان في صدر مملكته

it must sit like a Sultan in the midst of its dominion,[150]

وجعل الحضرة الإلهية قبلته ومقصده

and place the Divine Presence as its focal direction and its purpose,[151]

وجعل الآخرة وطنه وقراره

and place the HereAfter as its destination and its resolution,[152]

والنفس مركبه، والدنيا منزله، واليدين والقدمين خدامه، والعقل وزيره، والشهوة

عامله، والغضب شحنته، والحواس جواسيسه

and the Soul as its vessel, and the world as its place of descent, and the hands and feet as its servants, and the Intellect as its Vizier, and the Concupiscent Faculty as its Administration, and the Irascible Faculty as its Defense Force, and the Senses as its spies.[153]

---

149 The favor granted to man to become a *'Khalīfah'* as we discussed in Chapter 3

150 Like the King on his throne, with his palace at the center of the City, from whence he governs his Kingdom.

151 This is your Purpose of *Being*, or Purpose of Existence, the "why you were created". You were created but to *Know* your Lord and to hold utmost trust and conviction in Him, Exalted be He.

152 This is your Purpose of Life, the "why you were sent to earth". You were sent here to cultivate your HereAfter, to prepare your being for an existence in eternity.

153 *Manzil* منزل means a place where the journeyman alights as a place of temporary refuge. I do not know of a more fitting translation other than "place of descent" since man was "Sent down" to earth, or the material realm, which is his *Manzil* منزل, and he is, in this realm, a traveler until he continues his journey forward to the next destination, the HereAfter. To elaborate further using an allegory, a man visited a sage who lived in room devoid of any furnishing. He asked, "Where is all your furniture?" The sage asked, "Where is yours?" The man said, "I do not need any as I am just a traveler." The sage said, "As am I. We are all but temporary residents renting this earth from its Owner."

وكل واحد موكل بعالم من العوالم يجمع له أحوال العوالم

And each one of these has been entrusted a domain from the domains collectively to (partake in) the states of the domains.[154]

وقوة الخيال في مقدم الدماغ كالنقيب يجمع عنده أخبار الجواسيس

And the Imaginative Faculty is in the frontal lobe of the Brain. Like the 'Chief,' it gathers with it all the information (received from) the 'Spies' (senses). [155]

وقوة الحفظ في وسط الدماغ مثل صاحب الخريطة يجمع الرقاع من يد النقيب ويحتفظها إلى أن يعرضها على العقل

And the Recollective Faculty is in the center of the brain. Like the 'Map Master', it gathers what the Chief has and preserves it to be presented to the Intellect.[156]

---

154 Again, this has to be understood in the Arabic because the translation, without an explanation, does not do it justice. What it essentially means is that each of these faculties mentioned has been given a part of the being's dominion, a designated constitution and a role to play that collectively contributes to the overall health of the being, physically, mentally, and spiritually.

155 He is now speaking about the Brain as the primary inroad of information and how that information is delivered to the Mind, or the Intellect, for interpretation. This is a vital piece because the brain as the body's central processor is responsible for regulating optimal biological states, as well as the point of entry for everything the senses receive. This includes what the being experiences in the material reality, what it hears, sees, and senses. The anatomical term for this faculty would be the 'Neo-Cortex' or the 'Frontal Lobe'. One must also understand here that the Brain does not collect knowledge, neither do the senses. Both of these only collect information. The eyes collect visual information, whereas the ears collect auditory information, and likewise for all the other senses. The Brain in this regard computes that information, to categorize all the raw data into comprehensible images, or symbols, that the Intellect can interpret.

156 Memory is simply defined as the continued retention of information over time. In the Brain, this function is fulfilled by neurons firing in different variations, and over time these variations become set algorithms, such that each variation triggers its specific recollection. Here we must distinguish between Memory and Recollection. The memory itself is not stored in the Brain, rather it is stored in the Heart. When the Brain recognizes known patterns in the information it receives, the Intellect is able to associate those patterns to what is already known and stored in the Heart. This is the 'Recollection,' and the Memory itself is a 'known entity' recalled from the Heart.

148

فإذا بلغت هذه الأخبار إلى الوزير يرى أحوال المملكة على مقتضاها

When (in this manner) the information reaches the Vizier, he is able to evaluate the states of the dominion accordingly. [157]

فإذا رأيت واحداً منهم قد عصى عليك، مثل الشهوة والغضب، فعليك بالمجاهدة،

ولا تقصد قتلهما، لأن المملكة لا تستقر إلا بهما

If you see that any one from them are revolting against you, such as the Concupiscence or Irascibility, then upon you is the struggle (to suppress the rebellion) but not to destroy them. Because the dominion cannot be stabilized without them.[158]

فإذا فعلت ذلك كنت سعيداً، وأديت حق النعمة، ووجبت لك الخلعة في وقتها،

وإلا كنت شقياً، ووجب عليك النكال والعقوبة.

If you do that, you will be content, and you will fulfill the right of that favor. And in time, the robe of honor will descend upon you. And if not, you will be damned, and upon you will be chastisement and punishment.[159]

This is what Ghazzālī calls *'The Alchemy of Happiness.'* His argument is simple enough to understand. That the Being has been placed inside a Heart, which is placed inside a Soul that facilitates its link to the Body which is of the realm in which the Being was destined to be. And the Heart is disposed to seek out a contentment for the Being who is, by his nature, in a perpetual state of agitation because he is innately helpless.

---

157 As we said the Brain computes information, and the Mind, or the Intellect, interprets that information by associating Symbol (informative) with Meaning (knowledge). Here, a sound mind will only interpret what is received by the Brain, and not make assumptions that are contrary to reality. In the cases where the mental state is not sound, like a disorder, or even intoxication, the mind is said to be deluded, either because what the senses are accumulating does not match reality (delusion from the biological side, such as through a substance), or the mind has an internal conflict (delusion from the psychological side, such as through disorder or complex).

158 You, the Being, that is in the Heart. Revolting against you means they, the inclinations of the Self are doing other than your Will or Intent, where your Will and Intent are sound and sincere.

159 You will become the *Khalīfah* He intended you to become. That is the honor in fulfillment of your created purpose.

And he is helpless because he did not originate himself, and cannot do anything to prevent his own annihilation. Rather he can do nothing in absoluteness by his own volition, much like the infant that cannot cleanse nor feed itself, let alone conquer the world. The Being needs a nurturer, for he has been created to be dependent on the *only* One who can save and sustain his existence. Thus the Being's true contentment is in the assurance of the longevity of his existence, which he must eventually realize can *only* come from المقيت the *Sustainer Himself*. There is no true refuge or solitude wherever he may search it, save that he will find it in the embrace of الصمد the Everlasting Protector. And this means that the Heart's only real purpose is fulfilled by *Knowing* the Lord with innermost understanding, and *Believing* in the Lord with utmost trust and conviction.

It can only achieve this purpose through the seeking of purified knowledge, which can only be achieved when it is freed of the shackles of the realm it exists in. It must then take charge.

You, the being, must take charge of your dominion.

Remember who you are. Remember where you have come from. Remember what your destiny is. Recognize what your troops are. Strive to discipline and put them in their proper places, so that they may serve you, and not control you. For if they control you, then you are their slave. And if you are their slave, you cannot be a slave of Allāh. And if you cannot be a slave of Allāh, you cannot be freed from everything else. And if you cannot be freed from everything else, you will never realize true freedom. And if you cannot realize true freedom, you will never taste true contentment. And thus you will become a wretched being.

How then can you expect the robe of honor to descend upon you?

How then can you expect to become the *Khalīfah* that He wants you to become?

For if you will not strive to fulfill the purpose of your being *here and now*, when then will you do it?

MORE BOOKS BY ABUBILAAL YAKUB

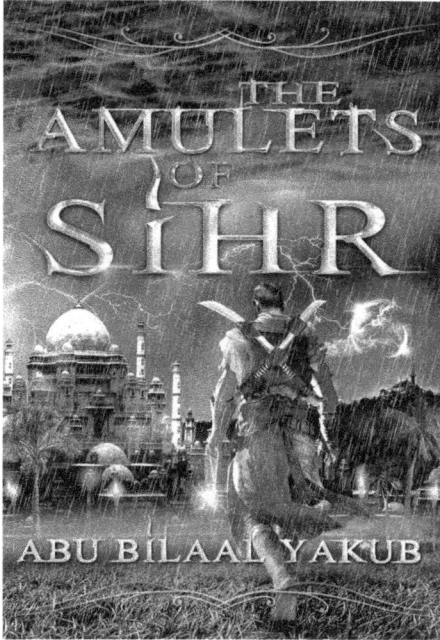

THE AMULETS OF SIHR

Part One of a Four-Part Fictional Series.

Mukhtar's life is upturned when he uncovers a dark secret concealed by his father.

Life is brutal and harsh, even harsher while the empire only looks after its own, and the rest of the people are left to fend for themselves. In an impulsive moment Mukhtar frees four slaves from their captors. Little does he know how this would shape his destiny. As the turmoil unfolds, his mother unveils her most guarded secret - an ancient and powerful amulet once belonging to his long-lost father. The Amulet sets Mukhtar on a path to unraveling a grim and dark part of his bloodline.

Now, at the crossroads of good and evil, he must face his life's greatest trials in order to save the empire from annihilation.

Enter the realm of the Unseen...

Prepare to face the evil beyond the veil...

THE EYE OF KIBR

Part Two of the Fictional Series.

Mukhtar's tale continues as he sets out to right the wrongs of his father.

As the King lies on his deathbed, the Empire hinges on the whims of his successors while evil forces both from within and without conspire to conquer the world of man.

Mukhtar's brother, Zaki, establishes himself with the Crowned Prince, while Mukhtar, displeased with his brother's bureaucratic approach, takes matters into his own hands to find a resolution to the crises.

Along the lines, those whom they thought were their enemies are discovered to be mere pawns of an ancient order known as the Hidden Ones attempt to restructure civilization to their liking, all the while following the whispers of the Hand of Azazil who is on the cusp of breaking free from his bonds.

THE DIVINITY OF TIME AND COSMOLOGY

Part One of a series titled *The Impostor and The Two Tribes,* an abridgment of the much larger philosophical work entitled *Time, Light and Being.*

In a devious ploy of secularizing and institutionalizing education and academics, from childhood to adulthood, for generation after generation, the Modern Age has thus far succeeded in the secularization of the Golden Knowledge of Islamic Sciences. It is upon us, the Muslims, the Believers, to revive the Golden Age of Islamic Knowledge and Sciences by revisiting the Knowledge of the Holy Qur'an and Hadīth.

This book begins with the beginning, with the Elements of Creation, Time, Light and the Cosmos, with the hopes of enabling the Believer with the ability to see with his inner eye, and pierce through the Dajjalic veils of the Modern Godless Age.

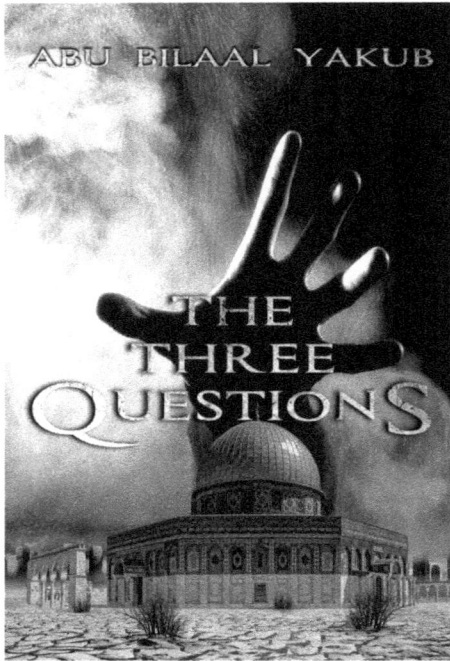

THE
THREE
QUESTIONS

Part Two of a series titled *The Impostor and The Two Tribes,* focusing on a unique unfolding during the Holy Prophet's time, which resulted in the Revelation of the anchor of *Islamic* Eschatology in the Holy Qurān

Close to the end of the Third Meccan Period, between 619 and 622 AD, in a desperate attempt to foil the unstoppable spread of *Islām*, the Ruling Tribe of the Qur'aysh sent a delegation to the Rabbis of Yathrib, returning with Three pivotal Questions to test the Holy Prophet of God.

Three Questions that have sculpted the fate of mankind into the modern, secular age we live in today. This book explores these three questions to pierce the godless veils of deception, and better understand the strange unfolding of event in the world, hellbent on ushering the harbinger of evil, the Impostor Messiah, and the dawn of the End of Times.

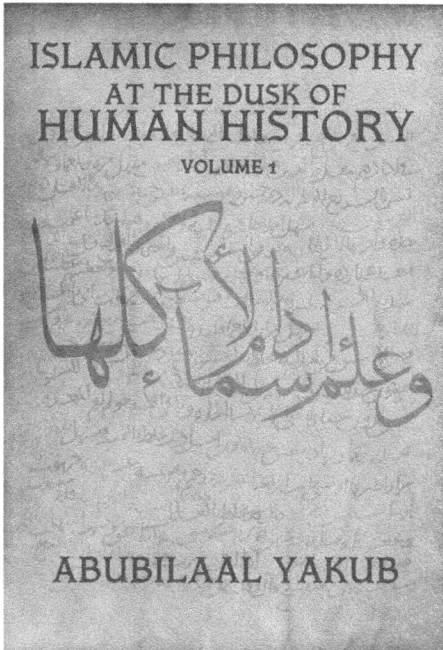

ISLAMIC PHILOSOPHY
AT THE DUSK OF
HUMAN HISTORY
VOLUME 1

ABUBILAAL YAKUB

ISLAMIC PHILOSOPHY AT
THE DUSK OF HUMAN
HISTORY vol.1

The first volume in a series that seeks to revive the true wisdom of Islamic Thought in an age deprived of it.

Philosophy, in the Muslim World, played an important role in cultivating deep and critical thinking to resolve queries into existential matters. In recent history, driven by certain influences, philosophy has been unjustly classified as *non grata*, deemed as something disapproved by Islamic doctrine.

Yet the world is shaped by philosophies unfounded in religious thought, rendered unchallenged to reign free. This series seeks to revive the critical thinking once beheld by the Muslim Civilization that challenges the ideologies of modernity.

ABUBILAAL YAKUB

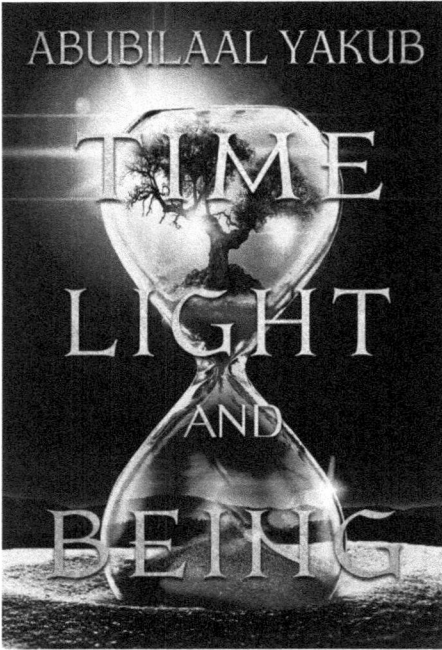

TIME,
LIGHT,
AND BEING

A philosophical work on the prime ontological elements that form the crux of existence for the human being.

Seldom does man think of his being, his purpose of existence, where he came from, where he is, who he is, and where he is destined.

Seldom does man think of his being, and what he is becoming.

Why did God create you?

Why are you here?

What does it mean "to be," and how does one realize the essence of being existent in Time?

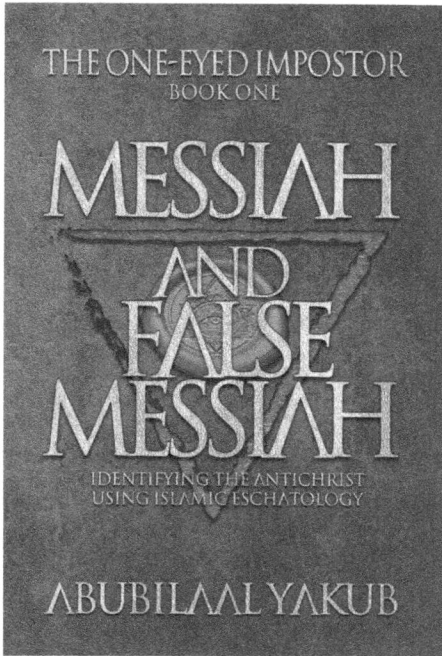

THE ONE-EYED IMPOSTOR

Book One

MESSIAH AND FALSE

MESSIAH

An Eschatological work focusing on the subject of the center-most figure in the End Times Eskhatos.

Humanity is no stranger to its finality. Only a fool is oblivious to the ultimate conclusion of man's existence in this world. Our acknowledgement of this as the bedrock of a strange transformation, unprecedented in human history, is that this is a manifest fulfillment of Divine Prophecy.

This book seeks to examine the central figure, described as the One-Eyed Impostor, the Dajjal, the Antichrist, whose prime role is to set the stage for the final act mankind will play before the curtain is drawn on human history.

abubilaal@ironheartpublishing.com

@abubilaalyakub

@abubilaalyakub

@abubilaalyakub

www.ingramcontent.com/pod-product-compliance
Lightning Source LLC
Chambersburg PA
CBHW022009080426
42733CB00007B/539